PUBLIC SPEAKING FOR ABSOLUTE BEGINNERS

Public Speaking for Absolute Beginners

SALLY JENKINS

ABOUT THE AUTHOR

Sally Jenkins is a member of Sutton Coldfield Speakers Club. Prior to joining the club in 2013, she hated and feared speaking in public. However, as an author, the ability to face an audience and promote herself was of vital importance. Sutton Coldfield Speakers Club helped Sally achieve confidence in public speaking and in 2018 she represented the Midlands in the national final of the Association of Speakers Clubs Annual Speech Competition.

Now Sally regularly evaluates the speeches of other club members, has represented the club in competitions and also gives those previously feared talks about her work as an author.

Find out more about Sally or contact her via her website https://sally-jenkins.com/.
Follow her on Twitter at @sallyjenkinsuk.

DEDICATION

With thanks to all the members of Sutton Coldfield
Speakers Club who have listened to me speak and
provided constructive criticism.

CONTENTS

WHY LEARN TO SPEAK IN PUBLIC?

"Wise men speak because they have something to say." – Plato.

Two types of people buy books on public speaking: the pantsters and the planners. Which are you?

Pantsters, as the name suggests, are flying by the seat of their pants. They have an immediate need to speak in public, for example, a wedding speech, a eulogy, a work presentation, a vote of thanks, a one-minute introduction at a networking event or election to the committee of a local organisation such as Rotary or the Women's Institute.

Planners are those who foresee they may need to speak publicly at some, as yet undefined, time in the future. This might be to motivate others, educate, promote their own business or charity or simply for their own self-development. These people do not yet have any speaking engagements but are working towards that goal.

This book can help you become a more confident speaker, whether you are a pantster or a planner.

Proficient, confident public speaking can't be learned overnight from a book; it takes many hours of preparation and, most importantly, follow-up practice in front of an audience. It also takes the ability to accept any feedback offered to you on your performance and to use that feedback to improve next time. At the end of this book is a list of organisations that offer a 'safe' environment in which to practise public speaking and receive constructive feedback. I recommend you visit one of these organisations to see how they might benefit you and then use them in conjunction with this book.

Learning to speak in public *before* the need arises, like the planners, is the least stressful way of becoming an effective public speaker. But if you're a pantster who's bought this book with only two days to go before a job interview requiring a presentation to a board of directors, do not despair; there is still time to read the whole of this book and digest the tips before you address your future employers.

Benefits of Learning to Speak in Public

The impact of learning and practising public speaking will go way beyond a dreaded single talk or presentation. The journey to confidence in front of an audience also brings the following benefits:

- The ability to speak concisely and persuasively

in meetings.
- Small talk with strangers becomes easier.
- Interaction with people at all levels is improved.
- Bravery levels increase and other things in life which previously seemed impossible now appear achievable.
- A more confident and positive attitude to life.

A friend recently told me how much I had changed since she first met me a few years ago. "You were so quiet," she said. "I never imagined you'd go around giving talks about your books. Now you're so confident in everything you do." I recognise that change in myself too. It began only a few months after joining Speakers Club. It became more pronounced once I'd got a couple of speaking engagements outside of the club under my belt. I still feel nervous at the start of a presentation, but as I sense the audience relaxing, I relax too and almost enjoy the experience.

It is said that many people fear public speaking more than death. Don't wait until the terror of that unwanted presentation is looming, learn to speak in public *now* and enhance *all* aspects of your life. It may even give you the confidence to ask your boss for a pay rise or a promotion.

This book will guide you through the skills needed to become a confident public speaker and provides tips on many common types of public speaking occasions.

Learning point: Confidence in public speaking will enhance your whole life. It is a skill worth acquiring.

Exercise: Note down the reasons why you want to become a confident public speaker. Put the list somewhere safe and refer back to it whenever your motivation wanes or you feel tempted to sidestep a speaking opportunity. These written reasons should keep you motivated when nerves or fear threaten to derail you!

BANISH THE DEMONS

"There are two types of speakers: Those who get nervous and those who are liars." - Mark Twain.

In 2014 YouGov did a survey in the UK about phobias. They presented respondents with 13 common phobias and asked them how fear-inducing they found each one. Fear of heights came top of the poll, with snakes and public speaking very close behind. Daily life in Britain rarely includes a meeting with a snake or a brush with altitude but there are many reasons why you might be called upon to speak in public. Forget heights and snakes, public speaking is the number one fear you need to conquer.

Who is most afraid when an unknown speaker stands up to give a presentation? Surprisingly, it is the audience. The audience is stepping into the unknown; they don't know what the speaker will say, they don't know his presentation style and they don't know if they have wasted their time turning up for the talk. This means the audience is always rooting for the speaker to do well and be entertaining – they want to get value from their ticket money and feel they haven't squandered an hour of their time on someone who mumbles or meanders without getting to the point. The speaker, on the other hand, is on safe ground. He knows both the content of his speech and what he is going to ask of the audience in terms of concentration or participation, plus his fee is in the bag. The speaker has the advantage. Next time you attend an event with a speaker, think about how you feel when he or she takes to the stage. At what point in the speech do you start to relax? Are you on the speaker's side, silently rooting for him to do well and giving him the benefit of the doubt if he appears hesitant or nervous? Remember, in most public speaking situations everyone, audience and speaker, is apprehensive and everyone wants the speech to go well. It is not a 'them and us' situation. Fear is natural but it shouldn't overwhelm you.

What can you do to feel more in control of yourself and the public speaking experience? Banish those demons that hold you back. By demons, I mean those little evil voices that whisper negative thoughts in your ear whenever you contemplate speaking in public. Thoughts such as: "You'll forget the words" "You'll be boring" "You'll stand there wringing your hands and looking stupid" and "You'll blush bright red like a beetroot." The following actions, without any further knowledge of public speaking or reading of this book, will go a long way towards exorcising these specific niggling demons:

- **Forgetting the words:** Spend adequate time on proper preparation and create brief bullet point notes to ensure you won't forget the words. Giving a speech is like an iceberg: 90% of the work is in the invisible preparation beforehand.

- **Being boring:** Match the content of your talk to the audience to keep them interested and wanting more.

- **Hand wringing:** Use hand gestures to emphasise particular points in your speech and be aware of keeping your hands in a neutral position the rest of the time to stop any fear of 'looking stupid'.

- **Blushing:** Some people blush easily and some people don't; it's a genetic thing. I am a blusher and when I finish speaking, I am often red-cheeked. There's nothing I can do about it, so I've stopped worrying. Red cheeks haven't stopped me winning speech competitions and selling books at the end of my author talks.

All the above demons relate to self-consciousness. In order to speak in public successfully, self-consciousness must be switched off or minimalised. The easiest way to do this is to change the focus of your mind away from you and towards the audience. Redirect your thoughts to the listeners and the message you are trying to give them. It's easier to be friends with an unselfish person whose first thoughts are for those around them. Similarly, it's easier to listen to an unselfish speaker who is focussing on the needs of his audience rather than on how he feels himself.

Visualisation

The one thing that has most helped me banish the demons of public speaking is *positive visualisation*. When I practise a speech at home, I visualise it being a success. I imagine I have an audience in front of me. I let my eyes roam over my imaginary listeners and I build up a rapport with that audience. I imagine myself talking fluently and engaging the interest of those before me.

Too often when we want to achieve something we see only the obstacles in our path. These obstacles grow to gargantuan proportions in our minds and stop us taking any action to move forward. Instead of dwelling on the barriers to success, concentrate on enjoying that success.

Boxing legend, Muhammad Ali, mentally rehearsed every fight before entering the ring. He imagined the crowd celebrating his victory at the end of the contest. Similarly, when he was still trying to make it big, actor Jim Carrey visualised himself being a great star. You must visualise yourself as a confident public speaker in order to become a confident public speaker.

The visualisation technique can be further broken down into three parts:

- **Outcome Visualisation** – imagine the successful delivery of your speech. Hear your name being announced as you walk to the podium, stage or lectern. See the view from that stage and think about what you'll be wearing. Hear the applause from the receptive audience. Visualise yourself speaking slowly, confidently and calmly using lots of eye contact.

- **Method Visualisation** – visualise the individual steps needed in the process to reach the above successful outcome, for example, research into your speech topic, note making, condensing those notes into bullet points, timing the length of the speech, practising alone and/or at your speakers club and so on. Visualise yourself spending a little time every day working on the speech so that it becomes a habitual part of your daily routine. Make this vision as clear and specific as possible, for example see yourself researching on the laptop for 15 minutes each lunchtime for the first week of preparation, in the second week visualise yourself converting research notes into a logical speech for 15 minutes each day, in the third week visualise the rehearsal process in your lounge at home. Method visualisation has been shown to make people start their preparation tasks earlier and to stick with them on a regular basis until the event itself.

- **Back-Up Plan Visualisation** – do *not* visualise failure but do give yourself extra confidence by visualising how you will recover if things were to go wrong during the presentation. For example, what if the technology fails? Do you have a hard copy of your presentation? Do you have a backup of the slides? If your mind goes blank, do you have some bullet point notes in which you can easily find your place? Imagining yourself coping when things go wrong in a speech will stop nagging worries at the back of your mind. But imagining failure is not an option!

Performer Mode

Some public speakers cope with nerves by stepping into 'performer mode' as they walk onto the stage or up to the lectern. Like an actor stepping into character, they take on the persona of a bigger, brighter version of themselves. Doing this can feel like putting on a protective cloak to face the audience. This 'cloak' enables the speaker to be more daring and dramatic than he or she ever would be in real life. Performer mode allows you to be the star of the show even if you are an extreme introvert in real life. Practise putting on the cloak when practising the speech at home.

Learning point: Anxiety about public speaking is natural. Minimise it by seeking solutions to specific worries. Practise positive visualisation or pulling on the protective cloak of 'performer mode' before you stand up to speak.

Exercise 1: Write down the aspects of public speaking that scare you the most. Use a different colour ink to note against each point how you will overcome that fear.

Hint: it should be possible to overcome most fears by preparation or practice.

Exercise 2: Practise the three-part visualisation process as you approach your first speech. During the outcome visualisation process, practise pulling on your performer mode cloak.

LIMBERING UP

You've made the decision to speak in public, or maybe it's been made against your wishes by higher powers. Either way, there's a lot of preparation ahead, but before we go any further, we need to do some preparatory limbering up, in the way that athletes jog gently before a race. When addressing a group of people, your voice needs to become larger than life, in volume, clarity and tone variation. Some people find it harder than others to make the necessary adjustments to their speaking range, but practice can improve everyone's performance. The exercises described here are particularly important for any of you who dislike drama, are quietly spoken or have speaking idiosyncrasies, but all public speakers should try them in order to further improve their speech delivery.

Breathing

When I first started speaking in public, I dismissed the need to breathe properly, thinking it didn't really matter. I changed my mind when I attended a workshop on performance skills for authors. The workshop focused on reading aloud and made me realise that proper breathing *does* matter. When it was my turn to read, the tutor criticised me for taking many shallow breaths during the reading of my piece. These breaths interrupted the flow of the narrative, limited how far I could project my voice and meant I lost volume at the end of sentences.

Most of the time we breathe shallowly in the upper chest area only. This causes the chest to rise and constricts the rib cage, throat and mouth, i.e. it limits the effectiveness of the mechanism we need for speaking. It also means we need to breathe more frequently, which becomes obvious to the audience if our pauses for breath fall in the wrong place. The breathing needed for public speaking is deeper than everyday breathing and comes from the diaphragm.

Performance or diaphragmatic breathing requires practice:

- Rest one hand on your chest and one on your stomach.
- Open your mouth a little.
- Pull in your stomach muscles and push out all the air you can through your mouth. The hand on your stomach should move inwards.
- Relax the stomach muscles. Air will automatically come back in and the hand on your stomach will move outwards. This outward movement is caused by the dome-shaped diaphragm muscle flattening when the lungs above it expand. This flattening of the diaphragm pushes out the stomach muscles.

- Let this breath out whilst speaking, as though the breath is transporting your words.

It is difficult to get used to this new way of breathing but, once mastered, your voice should sound stronger and more confident. Plus, there are some additional benefits. This breathing technique:

- Encourages the speaker to stand up straight.
- Slows the heart rate and therefore has a calming effect.
- Makes the speaker appear more confident.

Practise this breathing technique for a few minutes every day so that by the time you need it for public speaking it's second nature.

Voice Projection

Unless you are addressing packed halls, most of your public speaking is likely to be without a microphone; therefore you need to get used to projecting your voice to the deaf old lady at the back of the room. A speaker who mutters down to his or her shoes is wasting everybody's time. After one speaking event an audience member chatted to me as I packed my things away ready to leave. He congratulated me on my talk, not because of the content (he wasn't interested in the sort of books I write) but because, unlike one of the earlier speakers, he could hear every word I said. "You didn't keep getting quieter towards the end of sentences," he told me.

To improve your voice projection, stand at one end of the biggest room in your house or flat (you might be less self-conscious if you do this when you are at home alone rather than with your partner or family). Breathe as described above and let out a long, loud AHHH (rhymes with 'bar') sound. Repeat this but making a loud MMMMM sound and then alternate the two. Now try projecting real words such as the months of the year, the colours of the rainbow or days of the week. Speak slowly and push your voice to the back of the room. You are aiming to achieve volume (without shouting) and clarity. Recognise and remember how this feels - you will need to replicate it when you are speaking to be heard in public.

Clarity

Speaking clearly is easiest when the vocal mechanisms of the mouth such as tongue, hard palate and soft palate, are well exercised. Tongue twisters provide good material for encouraging flexibility in this area. Remember to also project while reciting the rhymes. Start slowly, loudly and clearly, then gradually increase the pace but maintaining volume and clarity.

Some example tongue twisters to try:

Red lorry, yellow lorry. (Repeat faster and faster ad infinitum)

Peter Piper picked a peck of pickled peppers
A peck of pickled peppers Peter Piper picked
If Peter Piper picked a peck of pickled peppers

Where's the peck of pickled peppers Peter Piper picked?

How much wood would a woodchuck chuck if a woodchuck could chuck wood?
He would chuck, he would, as much as he could, and chuck as much wood
As a woodchuck would if a woodchuck could chuck wood. (Robert Hobart Davis and Theodore F. Morse)

You know New York, you need New York, you know you need unique New York. (Repeat)

Voice Modulation and Expression

A speech delivered in a monotone and at a single speed will send the audience to sleep. To maintain interest and enjoyment in a presentation, a speaker should vary the pitch, pace, volume and emotion of their voice to suit the content of the speech. (See also the section on Avoiding Monotony later in this book.) Depending on your everyday conversational vocal range, this can be easier said than done. I struggled with the Use of Voice assignment in the manual of the Association of Speakers Clubs. Varying the pace, volume and emotion in a speech, I can manage, but I find it very difficult to modulate my pitch.

To practise voice modulation and expression, choose contrasting paragraphs from a book or magazine to read aloud, or write something appropriate yourself. One piece should be exciting and the other solemn. Or pretend that you are commentating on a fast-moving local derby football match and follow it up by an imaginary, respectful commentary on the funeral of a head of state. In all cases try to inject voice modulation and expression and get used to how it feels to speak in a more dramatic way than usual. To get started, try the following two paragraphs:

"The gentle waves lapped up the beach of the desert island. Sebastian dozed in the sunny hammock strung between two trees. Wham! A thump between his shoulder blades upended the hammock and he hit the floor."

"Two cars raced each other through narrow streets, headlights blazing and horns in a permanent scream. The collision was a screech of screaming metal. And then silence. The silence that descends when no one lives. A dark silence punctuated only by a silver finger of moonlight."

The poet, Longfellow, advised actress, Mary Anderson, that to improve her voice she should, "Read aloud daily, joyous, lyric poetry." Joy and pleasure make the body relax, the action of the heart and lungs improves and the passages around the nose that control tone will open. So, try reading aloud something that makes you feel happy.

Idiosyncrasies

Some speech habits are readily accepted in general conversation but can become irritating or make a talk difficult to follow for an audience listening continuously to the same speaker for 45 minutes or longer. Ask a friend to tell you or record your own voice and see if you unconsciously have any of the following habits:

- Dropping the final consonant of a word. For example, it's common to say 'yeah' instead of 'yes' or 'bu' instead of 'but'.
- Dropping the initial 'h' sound from the beginning of words such as 'ouse' instead of 'house' or 'ere' instead of 'here'.
- Replacing the 'th' sound at the beginning of words with 'f' so that 'thing' becomes 'fing'.
- 'R' sounds at the beginning of words being made into 'w' so that 'red' becomes 'wed'.

If you find that any of the above is a problem that can't be corrected by concentrating on the way you speak, it may be beneficial to book a session with an elocution teacher.

Learning Point: The voice is the public speaker's most important tool. Think of it like a painter's brush, a wood carver's knife or an embroiderer's needle. It must be kept in top condition and ready to adapt to the delivery of a range of different words and emotions.

Exercise: Every day for a week practise the breathing and speaking exercises given in this chapter. Keep a log of time spent and any perceived progress. Use Method Visualisation (previously mentioned in the chapter 'Banish the Demons') to help maintain this daily habit into the future. Visualise how the exercises will fit into your daily routine. Before breakfast? Waiting for the kettle to boil? On the drive to work?

SPEECH CONTENT AND CONSTRUCTION

A good speech should be long enough to cover the subject but short enough to maintain interest.

Very Important Tip: Speak about subjects you feel passionate about. A speaker's obvious passion brings the topic alive for the audience. If you have to speak about a subject that doesn't interest you (perhaps for work), try to find a different angle of approach to help you 'sell' it to the audience and yourself. If you're not enthused by a topic, your audience won't be either. Look for a little known fact related to the topic or research some element of the subject that does light your fire. I struggled to get enthusiastic about a work presentation on the subject of our internal collaborative Wiki website. Whilst preparing the talk I discovered that Wiki is short for WikiWikiWeb and that 'wiki' means fast in Hawaii; thus a Wiki is a 'very quick website'. Wiki became a recognised term when it was added to the Oxford English Dictionary on March 15th, 2007. These facts aren't exciting, but they did enable me to construct an introduction to my presentation which had a bit more life than simply focussing on the wholly technical subject at hand.

There are three important points to bear in mind when deciding what content to include in your speech:

1. **Less is more.** People will only remember a small percentage of what you say; therefore a fact-packed speech will not lead to a better-informed audience. Include only the most important facts and deliver them in the most memorable way.

2. **Minimal use of notes makes for a better speech.** Talks delivered with the least use of notes have the most impact. Think about it – would you rather watch someone reading pages of fact heavy A4 or talking passionately and, seemingly, off the cuff? Again, this means fewer facts are better.

3. **The content should be something your audience is interested in.** This might not be the case if it is an 'enforced' work presentation, in which case it is your job to capture the audience's interest.

Points one and two indicate that the *delivery* is far more important than having heavy factual content in your speech. Constructing a speech wisely will make it both easier to deliver and simpler to remember without the use of copious notes.

Point three may mean thinking laterally about your

subject to ensure the interest of your audience. Have a brainstorming session. Think about how the audience might benefit from listening to you and how your subject is relevant to that audience. For example, if you are a builder, a general audience might not be interested in a presentation on bricklaying techniques per se but their interest could be captured if the talk is angled to teach them how to get the best value for money when having an extension built on their house and how to avoid cowboy builders. Think about what you can tell the audience that is new, surprising or intriguing. A speech about church bell ringing might gain the interest of an audience if you start by telling them that a few of their favourite celebrities such as Alan Titchmarsh, Jo Brand and Victoria Wood are known to have rung bells.

"Tell them what you are going to tell them, tell them and then tell them what you have told them."

I have seen the above quote variously attributed to Aristotle, Churchill and Dale Carnegie but whoever first said it, it is essential advice for the novice speaker constructing his first speeches. As you gain experience and confidence, you may wish to deviate from this rule but for now we'll stick with it.

The basic building blocks of speech construction go back to the infant school rules for writing a story. Every speech should have a beginning, a middle and an end. To reinforce the message of the speech, the beginning should indicate the topics that the speech will cover, the middle should cover those topics and the end should summarise what the speech has covered.

A speaker wants the audience to remember the content of his or her speech. Three techniques can be used to ensure that as much of your presentation as possible is remembered:

- Sequence the speech appropriately. The first and last parts of a speech are the best remembered. The middle of a talk is the least well recalled. Don't hide the most important fact in the midst of everything else.

- Make connections between the key points in your speech, i.e. instead of scattering disparate facts try to pull the facts together in some logical way so that, as you are delivering the speech, the memory of one fact will trigger the memory of another and thus you will remember what you have to say next. A speech structured chronologically is good for this.

- Make the audience work. If the audience has to think, they will remember the content of your speech better. Pose questions to the audience and ask them to raise their hands in a vote before you give them the answer. During the conclusion get the audience thinking about what you have told them. If they have to mentally recap what they've heard, they will remember it better.

The next three sections of this book will cover beginnings, middles and ends of speeches.

Learning Point: Having too many facts in a speech will mean nothing is remembered and make it harder to deliver. Make the content audience-appropriate and deliver it with minimum use of notes.

Exercise: Choose a subject you are passionate about or use a subject you have already been given to speak on by your employer. Brainstorm the five most important points associated with the subject and arrange them in a logical fashion. Choose an angle into the subject that will interest your audience and grab them from the very start.

BRILLIANT BEGINNINGS

**"You never get a second chance to make a great
first impression." – Actor Will Rogers.**

The first few sentences of a speech dictate whether the
audience will engage with the rest of what you have to
say. It is essential to hook them in the first minute or
they'll drift in and out of the presentation, not paying
attention.

Here are seven tried and tested ways of beginning a
speech:

- A startling statistic, for example, 97% of
  people hate their day job.

- An arresting quote, such as, "'I have planned
  the perfect murder," says Mr. John Smith.'

- Take a quick straw poll relevant to the subject
  of your speech, for example, "Put up your
  hand if you've ever been in love."

- Suggest a 'what if' scenario to get the audience's imagination working, such as 'What if all of us had enough private income to have no need to work for a living? How would the world function?'

- Open with a problem that must be solved. Choosing a problem relevant to the whole audience will be most effective. An audience of millennials (i.e. those born in the 1980s and 90s) or the parents of these younger people will be immediately interested if you begin, "One-third of millennials will never own their own home. How can you ensure that you will be one of the two thirds that do get on the property ladder?"

- Be humorous. This doesn't mean telling a joke. Jokes have a danger of falling flat, especially if they are inappropriate for the audience. A good humorous start to a speech could be a short funny story at your own expense, relevant to the rest of the content of the presentation.

- Use a visual aid to spark the audience's attention. I begin one of my author talks by holding up two books, *Pride and Prejudice* by Jane Austen and my psychological thriller *Bedsit Three*. I say, "These two books were written two hundred years apart, but they have one very important thing in common." I promise to reveal that very important thing to the audience later in the talk.

Whatever opening you choose, it must enable you to move smoothly into the main body of the speech, i.e. no 'forced' connections.

Signposting:

Having grabbed the audience's attention, the next step is to drop in a 'signpost' indicating how you are going to develop the rest of the presentation. Like glancing at a map before a long journey, signposts help to make the audience feel comfortable. They know in what direction the speech is going and this will help them remember the content. Below are some examples of signposting:

- I'm going to give you five things you can do to improve your current working life without the upheaval and uncertainty of changing jobs.

- I'm going to tell you about three so-called 'perfect' murders and discuss the flaws in their planning and why the perpetrators were eventually caught.

- I'm going to explain the basics of divorce law and tell you how much you can do for yourself to avoid large solicitors' bills.

- Despite having no sight or hearing, Helen Keller lived an eventful life. We are going to follow her journey from difficult child to accomplished adult.

Speech Beginnings to Avoid

- Don't say you aren't the right person to be giving this talk or that you haven't had time to prepare. This is disrespectful to the audience who have given up their time to listen to you.

- Don't start with a shopping list of the speech contents. The only impact this has is to signal to the audience that boredom is approaching.

- Don't apologise, unless you arrive late (ensure this doesn't happen by allowing extra time for your journey) or have developed a problem with your voice such as a bad throat or persistent cough, in which case take appropriate lozenges with you to ease the situation.

Eye Contact

Eye contact with the audience should be evident throughout a speech but it is mandatory in the first few seconds. Do not open a speech reading from notes. Open a speech by directing your gaze across the whole audience and speaking from memory. This acknowledges the presence of the audience and begins that all-important rapport building.

Learning Point: A speaker has less than a minute to grab the audience's attention. You must make an immediate impact both physically with your eyes and body language, and also with the content of your speech.

Exercise: Write two different openings to your speech using the methods described above. Practise them aloud, in front of your family or a friend if possible, and select the one you feel works best. Add one or two sentences to this beginning to signpost the audience about what is coming next (the signposting can be changed later if your speech takes a different course during its construction).

MAGNIFICENT MIDDLES

"The success of your presentation will be judged not by the knowledge you send but by what the listener receives." – Lilly Walters, professional speaker.

The middle of a speech is where many speakers fail. The typical speaker is a specialist in his subject and wants to share all of his knowledge with the audience. He reels off lists of dates, statistics, names and facts. The audience goes home shell-shocked and unable to remember a single thing they've been told.

The average attention span for an audience listening to an averagely interesting speech is only five to ten minutes. This is bad news for the speaker allocated a 45-minute speaking slot. It means the speaker has to produce a better than averagely interesting speech. If the speech is better than average and the audience is interestingly engaged, that attention span can stretch to a maximum of twenty minutes. It's no coincidence that TED talks are eighteen minutes long.

So those of us billed to speak for longer than twenty

minutes have a problem. How to keep the audience engaged for the whole of our speech?

This can be done by building a 'soft break' into your speech. A 45-minute billing is the perfect opportunity for two twenty minute connected speeches plus five minutes for an introduction and conclusion. The transition from part one to part two of your speech will signal to the audience that they can take a breath and refocus themselves on a new subject or on a different perspective of the same subject. If, as a novice, you are worried about maintaining a twenty-minute attention span, break the speech down into even smaller chunks. I have built my author speech, "How to Make Money out of Murder" from four chunks:

- How to write a thriller
- Where writers get their ideas
- How I write my novels
- Working with a publisher

Interspersed within the talk are three short readings from my novel. I constructed the speech in this modular way for three reasons. Firstly, each section is around eight minutes long – the right length for practising in a slot at my Speakers Club. Secondly, if an engagement demands a different length of speech I can easily remove one of the sections or add in a section taken from another modular speech of mine. Thirdly, the start of each section brings with it a new burst of speaking energy from me and a chance to re-hook the listeners before they start brooding on the television programs they are missing.

Eleven tips for a magnificent middle:

- As discussed earlier in this book – select only the most important facts that you'd like the audience to remember. Up to five facts are enough for an eight-minute speech or an eight-minute module from a longer speech.

- Create 'word pictures' around each of these facts. This means painting an image in the minds of the audience that will embed the fact into their memory. For example, if the name of a particular general in a battle is one of your important facts, take some time to describe the physical attributes of the general. Is he tall or short? Does he have a beard? Is he well loved by his troops? Have the history books recorded any of his idiosyncrasies? Once the general is 'alive' in the minds of your audience, they will remember his name and how he behaved in the battle. This method has the added benefit of making the speech easier to deliver with minimum use of notes. You might bullet point the five facts but the word pictures will stick in your mind without notes and you will be able to deliver them fluently and expressively without referring to a fact-filled script.

- Tell a story. This is similar to the word picture technique described above. Audience interest is re-awakened when the speaker indicates he is going to tell a story. The story should, of course, be relevant to the content of the speech. The best stories are those that enable the audience to put themselves in the place of the characters in the story. Do this by including sensory and emotional details, such as the smell of warm vinegar on the chips wrapped in newspaper or the ricochet of shock as armed police broke down the door. Do not read the story from notes and do not learn it off by heart. Relive the story, in front of the audience, in your own words. The end of the story should make a point to the audience. For example, if you are speaking on behalf of a charity providing maternity care in the third world, don't just focus on anonymous statistics about maternal mortality. Instead, focus on the case of one mother and her birth experience. Make the audience feel the woman's pain, suffering and anxiety. At the end of the speech, the charity collecting tin will be heavier than if the presentation had only looked at broad statistics.

- Ensure the speech progresses logically. This helps the audience take in the subject matter and it also helps the speaker deliver the speech. A speech with a logical progression is easier to memorise and requires less dependency on notes.

- Wake the audience up occasionally. Raymond

Chandler was an American crime novelist and told budding writers that when the middle of their story got saggy and without impact, they should, 'send in a man with a gun'. In a crime novel, a man with a gun ups the ante and makes things more exciting. It's not advisable to pull a gun in the middle of a speech but it is a good idea to drop in a surprising fact or revelation. Delivered slickly with appropriate pauses immediately before and after, this will make the audience sit up and take notice, just as if a man with a gun had walked into the room.

- If the subject matter is very dry and appears to have little direct benefit to the audience, build in some benefit for them, even if you have to invent it! For example, a work presentation about the implementation of a new money saving, but essentially tedious, back office procedure could be enlightened by humorous asides about what could be done by the company with each chunk of money saved. With your tongue in cheek, suggest the implementation of step one of the new procedure will free up enough money for chocolate cake every Friday for all staff, implementation of step two will free up enough money to install a workplace paddling pool for use on hot summer days. It doesn't matter that these ideas are all pie in the sky and that the audience knows the monetary savings will simply improve the company's balance sheet, your suggestions will still raise a smile and lighten the atmosphere of the talk.

- Give the audience the right amount of mental challenge, without making them struggle to understand. For example, if you are using PowerPoint slides, avoid spoon-feeding the audience with lots of explanatory printed bullet points but, also, don't present them with over-complicated graphs which will make them give up trying to understand.

- Include the audience in the speech. This can be done in several ways depending on how much interaction you want to encourage. An easy way is to ask for a show of hands in order to take a straw poll. A more confident speaker might encourage a question and answer session part way through his talk. Recently I watched a talk by a man who had researched the people from a particular local street who had died in World War 1. He included the audience directly in his presentation. Prior to speaking about each fallen soldier, he requested a volunteer from the audience to come to the front and hold a sheet of paper displaying the number of the fallen man's house. By the end of the talk he had ten people standing at the front with numbers and this drove home to the audience the impact that World War 1 deaths had had on just one small stretch of road. It also made the audience feel part of the talk.

- Change your presentation style part way through the talk. If you are using presentation media, switch from PowerPoint to flip chart or whiteboard. When you are telling a story or painting a word picture, speak in a lively manner but, in contrast, deliver serious facts in a more measured way.

- Choose the words you will use in your speech carefully. Short, commonly used words are better than long words that might have the audience searching on phones for an online dictionary or zoning out of the speech altogether. Onomatopoetic words are particularly effective in a speech. These sound like the thing they are describing, for example, 'crash', 'bang' and 'clang'.

- When speaking with passion and if you are trying to convert the audience to your point of view, avoid weak expressions such as, 'I suppose', 'it seems to me' or 'perhaps'. To convince people of your ideas, you must speak with authority and positivity.

Learning Point: Variety is the best way to keep the audience engaged. All possible variables of a speech should be changed during its delivery. A change is as good as a rest.

Exercise: Write the middle section of your speech. Go easy on the facts and try to include a story or a word picture to illustrate some of the factual content.

Note down any ways that you might introduce variety into your speech.

EXCITING ENDINGS

"Don't wait for an inspired ending to come to mind. Work your way to the ending and see what comes up." - Andy Weir, science fiction writer.

The ending of a speech should be equally as dramatic as its brilliant beginning. The words that you want the audience to remember the most, should be those that you say last. The last words of a speech should send the audience home thinking, pondering, eager to act on any call to action or to share what they've learned with friends and family. A speech should *not* simply fizzle out, as though the speaker has run out of material. A definite ending tells the audience when to clap and doesn't leave an awkward silence when only the speaker knows he's finished but the audience doesn't realise it's the end until the speaker shuffles away from the lectern.

Some of history's most famous quotes were the last words of speeches:

In 1940, Winston Churchill said, 'Let us therefore brace ourselves to our duties, and so bear ourselves, that if the British Empire and its Commonwealth last for a thousand years, men will still say, "This was their finest hour."'

Martin Luther King's 1963 'I Have a Dream Speech' ended with the now well-known quotation, 'Free at last! Free at last! Thank God Almighty, we are free at last'. Incidentally, King took this quote from an old Negro spiritual song.

However, don't worry if you don't have a clever ending in mind as you start to write the speech. And don't delay preparing the speech until an ending pops into your mind because it probably never will without some effort. Brainstorming the beginning and middle sections of the presentation will often throw up some strong concluding remarks.

Five Ways to End a Speech

- **Bookend the speech**. Take the presentation around in a circle and at the end of the speech refer back to something from the introduction. For example:
  Speech Introduction: In a 2015 YouGov survey 60% of respondents indicated they would like to earn their living as a writer.
  Middle section contains information on how much

authors earn.

Speech Ending: Given those author earnings figures, if that YouGov survey was carried out again today, would *you* still vote to be a writer?

- **Summarise and give a call to action.** "I've told you about the three pitfalls of dying without leaving a will. If you don't want your life savings to end up in the pockets of the government, NOW is the time to contact a solicitor and draw up your will. Take a leaflet for details of how to arrange a no-obligation consultation with me. Don't leave the fate of your life savings to chance or luck."

- **Summarise and repeat the most important fact from your talk.** "As I said at the beginning, General Smith is the most over-looked leader in history. However, now you know about his heroic actions saving ten of his men from certain death at the Battle of Storyland in 1872, I hope your opinion of him has changed."

- **Use the title.** Ensure the title of the speech encapsulates its message in a short, sharp way. Use the title as the final words of the speech to drive the message home. For example, a speech on banning fox hunting might have the following title/closing words, 'End the Massacre of Wild Animals in the UK'. When using this method, it can be easier to write the speech conclusion (and thus the title) before the speech beginning and middle.

- **Use a quotation**. End the speech with a memorable quotation that will stick in the audience's mind. Example: A speech about the speaker's long road to success, littered with failures but intended to demonstrate that determination and hard work *will* lead to success, could be concluded using the following quote from Thomas A. Edison, "I have not failed. I've just found 10,000 ways that won't work."

Things to Avoid

- Being lazy and simply ending a speech with 'Thank you.'

- Ending your speech with, 'That's all I've got to say. Any questions?'

- Leaving loose ends. If you've mentioned something at the beginning of a speech, such as a quote or a statistic, be sure to refer back to it at the end in order to reinforce its significance and bring the speech full circle.

- Omitting any call to action. The general purpose of making a speech is to persuade. The speech can be funny and entertaining but the speaker wants the audience to respond in some way. The response might be in thought, word or deed. Think about what you want the audience to do following your speech. Remember the call to action from John F. Kennedy's 1961 U.S. presidential inaugural address: "Ask not what your country can do for you — ask what you can do for your country."

When devising the ending for your speech think about the music concerts you've attended (both pop and classical) and how, at those, the best tracks or songs are always saved until last in order to finish with a resounding finale. Do the same with your speech.

Learning Point: The speakers who are most remembered finish a speech with a bang. They leave the audience thinking and discussing.

Exercise: Think about the effect you want your speech to have on the audience. Do you want to change their point of view? Encourage a charitable donation? Educate them about a period in history? Brainstorm some strong endings for your speech that will drive home the effect you want.

GRIPPING GESTURES

When telling the truth, we make many hand gestures. When lying, our hands make far fewer movements.

What do you do with your hands in normal conversation? Are they stiff by your side or do they move around to emphasise particular points? Most people move their hands as well as their lips when they talk. When you are making a speech those hand gestures must be exaggerated and harnessed to work for you. Gestures, facial expression and the use of whole body language can greatly improve the effectiveness of a speaker's delivery. But too much hand or body movement without purpose can be distracting.

The following points give guidance on incorporating

meaningful gestures into a speech in a natural way and also provide tips on avoiding fuzzy gesture 'static':

- Avoid constantly moving your hands in a non-specific way. This is often described as 'accordion playing' because it looks like you're moving your hands in and out, as though playing the accordion. Hand movements or gestures should be reserved for illustrating a particular point. The rest of the time try cupping one hand in the other in front of you, with the arms at full length. Or simply have your hands by your sides.

- Avoid tightly clasped hands. These can inhibit free movement and make the flow into any gestures appear forced.

- Never put your hands in your pockets. This might seem like an easy way of keeping your hands still but it gives a lazy, over-relaxed impression of a speaker who isn't completely involved in his presentation.

- Don't hold a pen or other object while you speak. If you do, you will fiddle with it, passing it from hand to hand, turning it around and eventually drop it on the floor. All of this is annoying and distracts the audience from your message.

- Don't constantly shift your weight from one

foot to another or walk from one side of the stage to the other. This will annoy the audience. The walking can turn the speech into the equivalent of a tennis match where the audience has to keep turning their heads from side to side. The weight-shifting might give the audience a tendency to seasickness as the speaker's head bobs up and down like a seagull riding the waves.

- Following on from the above point, purposeful stepping to one side and then the other can work well if you are trying to put two sides of an argument. Each step to the left or right indicates a switch in the side of the argument being put forward.

- Lean forwards towards the audience if you want to give the impression that you are sharing a secret.

- In a large hall big gestures are needed to augment the speaker's words. In a small room the audience will be able to see facial and eye expressions and so less drama is necessary.

- Make sure your gestures can be seen by the audience. Don't make them where the lectern will obstruct the audience's view.

- Eye contact with the audience is important to make everyone feel part of the event. This counts as a gesture. Move your head to take in all parts of the room. You may find it easier to swivel from the hips to make sure you cover all the corners.

- Be careful with the timing of the gestures. As the speaker, you will have practised both words and gestures and know what's coming next. It's easy to fall into the trap of starting the gesture a split-second *before* you speak the words. This makes the gesture appear forced and false. Gestures must be timed to happen naturally with the spoken words as they might in conversation.

- Only use gestures that suit your style of speaking. Over the top dramatic gestures do not suit everyone.

- When practising at home, mark any specific gestures on the manuscript and incorporate them into each rehearsal.

For novice speakers nervous about the drama of incorporating large gestures into their speeches, the following are very natural movements and a good starting point for learning to speak with your hands as well as your voice:

- When you mention a number, emphasise it by holding up the correct number of fingers. For example, 'There are *four* steps to writing a novel.'

- Open your arms out wide when you describe something very large or move them close together to emphasise something small.

- Move your hand upwards to indicate growth or an increase, for example, an increase in the turnover or profit of a company. Move your hand downwards to illustrate a decrease.

- A clenched fist shows determination or deep strength of feeling.

Try not to consciously think about your gestures. They should be done subconsciously as in conversation. If your mind is on the gestures, it is not concentrating on the words or the meaning of your presentation and this will become obvious to the audience. Gestures are used to emphasise a point, they shouldn't look as though they have been tagged on simply to add some drama.

Facial expression can also be classified as a gesture. Matching facial expression to the emotion of the speech will increase rapport with the audience. Think of a stage actor who really lives his part – the expressions on his face help to pull the audience into his world. If you feel passionately about something, make sure your face reflects this and similarly if you find something distasteful or upsetting.

Learning Point: Talk with your hands as well as your voice to add emphasis to certain phrases. This will help with audience engagement. Don't forget the most important gesture of all – eye contact.

Exercise: Go through the manuscript of your speech and mark where specific gestures could be incorporated. Practise the timing of the gestures and the spoken words to make them appear as natural as possible.

AUDIENCE RAPPORT

Make the audience your friend.

Establishing a rapport with an audience means creating a relationship, building an understanding and generating empathy. The audience must be put at ease and made to feel comfortable as early as possible in a speech – hence the importance of a brilliant beginning. Once the spectators are on side, both they and the speaker will relax and enjoy the speech. When rapport is there, any lack of finesse in delivery will be overlooked. The speaker will give a better performance because an audience enjoying itself generates confidence.

There are many ways to go about building this elusive 'rapport':

- Chat to individuals as they arrive at the event before you take to the stage. Ask them about themselves as you might if meeting them at a party. This makes a connection and gets some audience members on your side before you even start to speak.

- Eye contact. A speaker who does not look at his audience will not build a relationship with them. Ensure the whole of the audience is included in your performance by scanning the room from corner to corner and front to back. If it's a big room do this by rotating from the hips rather than just moving your head. Make sure to include anyone sitting away from the main audience area such as a chairperson or secretary. If you fear direct eye contact, aim your gaze at people's foreheads, this is better than not focusing on the audience at all. To give sufficient eye contact, use only minimal notes. It's difficult to build audience rapport when reading from a script.

- When constructing and delivering your talk, remember that you have been invited there to serve the audience, not to give them a hard sell or impress them with what a wonderful person you are. Come at the talk from your audience's point of view. Consider their interests, problems and goals – how can you address these so they go home having learned something useful or fascinating? Don't blind them with science and jargon – they will be bored, not impressed with your knowledge.

- Don't be afraid to pause – the audience won't think you've forgotten the words! For example, asking a rhetorical question is a good way to build rapport but only if you pause to allow the audience time to think and the chance to agree or disagree with the question by nodding or shaking their heads.

- Tell a story. People like to hear a personal story. Personal stories can build an emotional connection.

- Dress appropriately, slightly smarter than you expect your audience to be is a good rule of thumb. This makes the speaker appear professional and confident. An audience relaxes more easily if the speaker appears to know what he's doing.

- Look interested, energetic and keen to speak. Audiences respond well to physical energy and enthusiasm and so be aware of your body language and gestures. Open gestures that reach out to the audience and draw them into the speech work particularly well. A speaker standing still with his hands in his pockets will not have the same rapport-building impact as a speaker swivelling from the hips with arms outstretched to pull in all the spectators.

- Use audience inclusive language, for example, 'all of us here know that …' rather than 'I know that …'

Many speakers find there is an interesting by-product from concentrating on audience rapport: the more the speaker concentrates on the needs of the audience, the less nervous, self-conscious and self-obsessed the speaker becomes.

Learning Point: Building a rapport with the audience makes for a more enjoyable experience for both audience and speaker.

Exercise: Practise your speech in front of a mirror and see yourself as the audience will. What are you doing through words and actions to draw them into your performance? Note down what you can do early in your speech to build rapport as soon as possible and mark these things on your manuscript.

PERFECT PAUSES

"The right word may be effective, but no word was ever as effective as a rightly timed pause." - Mark Twain.

Novice speakers are petrified of pauses. They gabble in order to get the whole awful public speaking experience over with as soon as possible. They fear that pausing for a few seconds will make the audience think they've forgotten the words, lost their place or run out of material. But fear not - audiences do not make any of these assumptions. Audiences like pauses. The use of pauses elevates an average speaker to a good speaker. When you pause you give the listeners time to process what you have just said and to prepare for whatever is coming next. Without pauses, a speech is delivered with the rapidity of machine gun fire and the audience will remember nothing of what you say.

If you naturally speak quickly it's even more important to incorporate pauses into your presentation. The confident use of pauses signals that the speaker is in control of the speech. Someone speaking in a rushed manner appears out of control. Imagine two politicians at the hustings. Politician One gabbles his way through the party's whole manifesto and Politician Two talks about only four points in the manifesto with several pauses. All other things being equal, which one would you vote for?

Two useful by-products of using pauses:

- The speaker needs less material to fill the same amount of allotted time.

- Pausing calms the speaker's terrified mind.

Types of Pauses

- **Punctuation Pauses.** Punctuation pauses act in the same way as a comma or a full stop in the written word. When people are listening to a speech they can't go back and re-read a sentence they didn't understand. The purpose of punctuation pauses is to allow the audience to make sense of what you are saying. These pauses should be brief and vary in length depending on whether they are taking the place of a comma or bridging the gap between two quite different sentences or paragraphs.

- **Dramatic Pause.** This type of pause does

what it says on the tin – it adds drama to the proceedings. A dramatic pause makes the audience focus on what you are about to say. For example, the phrase, "Guess what I found when I opened the rusty old trunk? *PAUSE*" That pause increases the tension and draws the audience into the speech by getting them thinking and anticipating what might be in the trunk. A dramatic pause is longer than a punctuation pause.

- **Reflective Pause.** With a reflective pause the speaker indicates out loud to the audience that he is explicitly leaving a few moments for them to think about what has been said. For example, the speaker might say, "It was the biggest natural disaster in a generation. Five thousand people died. Five thousand people - take a moment to think about that."

- **Pause for Humour.** Delivering humour is difficult (and is discussed in more detail in another section of this book) and mastering the pause before giving the punchline is essential. Study the performances of stand-up comedians and note how they use pauses to prime the audience before completing a funny story with the line that gets everyone laughing. Jokes take longer to register on stage than in conversation and therefore it's essential to use a pause to signal the punchline is coming and another pause afterwards to allow the audience to appreciate the joke.

- **Pause for Emphasis.** Use pauses to separate your main points. Use pauses to transition from one subject to another. Use pauses to vary the pace of your delivery.

- **Impression of Spontaneity Pause.** This is an advanced public speaking technique. It gives the impression the speaker is thinking about what he is saying, as though saying it for the very first time. In reality, the speaker may have given this same talk many times but the audience shouldn't feel as though he is just reciting by heart yet again. The speaker wants each audience to feel that the speech is fresh and new just for them. This can be done by introducing pauses during which it appears the speaker is thinking about what comes next.

- **Pause to Eliminate Filler Words.** Filler words are those we use to buy time whilst composing what comes next, for example 'um', 'er', 'like' and 'you know'. It's quite acceptable to need a second or two to think about what you're going to say next, but the constant use of filler words distracts from the message of the speech and makes it woollier and less defined. It's far better to pause than use a filler word. The speakers who use the least filler words are generally those who've done the most preparation and those who speak more slowly. Speaking more slowly means it's easier for the brain to keep up with feeding the words to the mouth.

Learning Point: Become comfortable with the sound of silence in your speeches. It will benefit both you and the audience.

Exercise: Find internet video clips of some of the best speakers of our time, such as Barack Obama, Martin Luther King, John F. Kennedy and current politicians. Listen for their use of pauses. Note down the purpose of those pauses and how that type of pause might be included in your speech. Go through the manuscript of your own speech and mark where a pause is necessary.

AVOIDING MONOTONY

Speaking by rote carries the danger of a monotonous delivery.

Most speeches are memorised, at least in part. However, speaking by rote lacks the rises, falls and shifts of emphasis in the voice that occur during natural conversation. This happens because the speaker isn't thinking about his words and their message as he speaks, he is concentrating on dredging up the paragraphs from his mind. Speaking by rote carries the danger of a monotonous delivery. A monotonous speech is one delivered at a single speed, at a single pitch and without inflection or emphasis. Imagine the sound of a voice synthesiser such as that used by the late Stephen Hawking. A monotonous speech lacks colour and vitality and will soon lose the attention of the audience. Listeners will become unsettled and will fidget and fiddle. A speech should be delivered with as much vocal energy, variation and colour as possible. In the preparation for your speech concentrate on varying your voice. Like a fingerprint, your voice is unique to you. Many of us now use our voice instead of a password to get access to telephone banking services. Don't try to change your voice. Instead, learn to use the whole of your vocal range to carry the audience's attention.

To avoid monotony try building the following speech variations into your talk:

Change of Pace

Pace or tempo is the speed at which a speaker delivers words. A tennis player knows that varying the speed of his serve will keep his opponent on his toes. Similarly, a bowler in cricket will send some balls fast and some slow. A composer will include many changes of tempo in his musical score. A speech in which some sentences are delivered rapidly and others at a more relaxed pace will keep the attention of the listeners. Changing the tempo makes the delivery of a speech sound more natural and less like speaking by rote (even if it is!). But the tempo change must be relevant to the context of the words. Compare delivering your speech to driving a car. In a car you must accelerate or brake according to the road conditions, as a speaker, you must speed up or slow down your delivery according to the meaning of different parts of the speech.

Speaking fast conveys excitement, energy and urgency.

Speaking slowly conveys thoughtfulness, seriousness, the delivery of wisdom or bad news.

The use of the pause (discussed elsewhere in this book) should also be considered when looking at the tempo of your speech.

Practice changing tempo by reading aloud. Children's stories can be particularly good for this, find one that contains both excitement (fast!) and more reflective (slow!) content.

Change of Pitch

Pitch is the highness or lowness of a speaker's voice. This is the thing that I find most difficult to vary in my own speeches but, done well, pitch variation can make a good speech outstanding. It's worth remembering that nervousness can cause the vocal cords to tense and shorten, thus making the natural pitch of your voice slightly higher.

A lower pitch demonstrates seriousness and authority.

A higher pitch can indicate excitement or surprise.

Practise varying the pitch of your voice by reading aloud a piece of text and speaking alternate sentences in a high pitch and then a low pitch so that your voice is forced to seesaw up and down.

Inflection/Modulation

Inflection or modulation refers to up and downward shadings of the voice within a single phrase. An upward inflection is a shift in pitch from low to high. A downward inflection is a change in pitch from high to low.

An upward inflection generally indicates a question, doubt or surprise.

A downward inflection generally indicates confidence or certainty.

Consider the phrase, "That's not bad" as a comment after tasting a home-baked cake. Saying it with an upward inflection towards the end indicates doubt, implying that the cake is acceptable but could be improved and the speaker is about to suggest how that improvement could be brought about. Saying the same phrase with a downward inflection towards the end indicates certainty, implying the cake is good and no suggestions for improvement are needed.

Tone

Tone of voice expresses a mood or emotion. In everyday conversation our tone of voice varies according to whether we are happy or depressed. Think about how you might say the phrase, "We've got something to tell you about Joanna" in two different circumstances. Firstly, when you're about to break the happy news that Joanna is expecting a baby, and secondly, when you're about to break the sad news that Joanna has been diagnosed with a terminal illness. Just as in natural conversation, when speaking in public the tone of your voice should change between the serious and more light-hearted parts of your speech.

Emphasis

When particular words in a sentence are emphasised, the sound of that phrase and sometimes its meaning, are changed. Emphasising a word indicates to the audience that they should take particular notice of that word because it has a bearing on the meaning of the whole sentence. Emphasis on a spoken word is equivalent to taking a fluorescent yellow highlighter pen to the written word. Think about the phrase, "I am now rich enough to go on a world cruise", emphasised in the following different places:

    a.   I am **now** rich enough to go on a world cruise.
    b.   I am now **rich** enough to go on a world cruise.
    c.   I am now rich enough to go on a **world** cruise.

Sentence 'a' indicates new riches. Sentence 'b' emphasises the wealth of the speaker. Sentence 'c' implies that previously the speaker could have afforded a shorter cruise.

Basic emphasis of a word can be achieved by speaking it more forcefully and this will go some way towards avoiding a monotonous delivery. Further emphasis can be achieved in the following ways:

- Pausing just before or after the phrase.

- Repeating the phrase (this will not avoid monotony unless you also use vocal emphasis of some kind as well). This is a technique advocated by Winston Churchill, he said, "If you have an important point to make, don't try to be subtle or clever. Use a pile driver. Hit the point once. Then come back and hit it again. Then hit it a third time - a tremendous whack."

- Body language – for example leaning forward slightly towards the audience as you speak to reinforce the importance of what you are saying (again, be sure to use vocal emphasis of some kind as well).

Think About the Meaning of the Words as You Speak

This is the single best way to avoid monotony in your speech, even if you are speaking by rote. Be convinced of the importance of the message you are trying to get across and be enthusiastic about getting this message over to your audience, each and every time you give the same talk. This conviction and enthusiasm will help you naturally inject the necessary variations in pace, pitch, inflection, tone and emphasis necessary to ignite that same passion and enthusiasm in your audience.

Learning Point: Even the most interesting speech content will soon bore an audience if delivered in a monotone. Monotony creates a restless audience.

Exercise: Use different colours of highlighter pen on your speech manuscript to indicate how you can vary pace, pitch, tone, modulation and emphasis. Practise these variations out loud. Record your speech and listen to how you sound.

MEMORISING VERSUS USING NOTES

Public reading is not public speaking.

There are four ways that speakers do/do not use notes to deliver presentations. Each has arguments for and against.

Reading the speech like an essay.

This is not really public speaking, it is public reading. Reading from a manuscript hinders a speaker's connection and rapport with the audience. Making eye contact or using gestures to emphasise a point is difficult. However, there are some circumstances when this might be necessary, for example, when it's important to use exact wording, maybe in a legal or other official context. An author giving a reading from his work may also read from a book or a document. Reading a speech may seem like an easy option requiring less advance practice, but be warned – holding the attention of an audience when reading aloud *does* require careful preparation! The section in this book on Reading Aloud gives some tips for the situation when a speaker finds himself having to read to an audience. But, whenever possible, avoid reading a general talk or presentation.

Learning the speech off by heart.

Learning a speech off by heart often makes it sound memorised, monotonous and regurgitated. Speeches delivered this way can lack emotion or power because the speaker is concentrating on recalling the correct words instead of getting the message across to the audience. There is another danger in learning by heart: if you forget a few words part way through the speech, you are likely to become anxious about finding the place in your memory from which to continue the speech and this can put the rest of what you have to say in jeopardy. Plus, it's time-consuming to learn something word for word. The only good thing I can say about learning the speech by heart is the delivery will be better than reading the speech like an essay.

Using notes to jog the memory about points to include in the presentation.

This is the most popular way of speaking and best for the beginner. It is also the way I approach any speech longer than around ten minutes (shorter than this I try to speak extemporaneously – see below). Use a list of bullet points to provide a pathway through the speech. These can be typed on a maximum of two sheets of A4 in a font size you can read easily without the need for reading glasses (using reading glasses makes looking up to make eye contact with the audience difficult). Two sheets are the maximum because these can usually be fitted side by side on a lectern, meaning there will be no need for the annoying activity of the speaker turning the pages of his notes. As you gain experience and confidence minimise the amount of notes needed and try to condense them onto index cards. Small cards are less obvious than A4 sheets of paper. Toastmasters International advocate using blue cards for notes because they are less distracting for the audience. Some people prefer to keep their notes digitally on a tablet, others fear a technology failure. Having to swipe the tablet screen awake to view the notes can be distracting for the audience and annoying for the speaker. Whatever the format of your notes, memorise the gist of what you will say to expand each bullet point but, for the reasons mentioned above, do not learn by rote – see the section below for how I achieve this.

Extemporaneously

(Note: this can refer either to an impromptu speech or a carefully prepared speech delivered without notes. In this section of the book we are referring to the latter definition).

This works best for shorter speeches which are not fact heavy. Practise using the following steps when preparing to give a speech extemporaneously:

a. Write the full manuscript of the speech.

b. Read the speech aloud a few times using the timer facility on your mobile or watch. This ensures the speech is the right length and will highlight which parts of the manuscript can be easily memorised, for example, where only the gist of a paragraph needs to be correct. It will also indicate which parts of the speech need more work to ensure an accurate delivery, for example, where the exact wording of a sentence is important because there is the use of alliteration or onomatopoeia.

c. Bullet point the speech and practice until the talk can be delivered using the bullet points only. The words you use on each run through will vary (except where exact wording is required) but as long as the gist is there, that's fine.

d. Continue to practise until the bullet points become redundant.

Using brief notes or speaking extemporaneously both require the speech topics to be *internalised* rather than memorised. This means knowing your subject so well that you can talk about it in many different ways, i.e. the gist of your speech will be the same each time but the actual words you use will differ. Speaking in this way gives greater flexibility to tailor your speech on the hoof to changed time requirements and audience interests. Plus, if you lose your place in the speech, it's easy to say to the audience, "Where was I?" and pick up from their cue.

Learning point: Presenting using fewer notes requires more preparation but leads to a better performance.

Exercise: Break your speech down into the minimum number of bullet points necessary to deliver it from internalised (not rote!) memory with no reading aloud.

READING ALOUD

"The book which you are reading aloud is mine, Fidentinus; but, while you read it so badly, it begins to be yours." – Marcus Valerius Marshall, Roman poet.

If you are an author, poet or playwright, you may be asked to read your work aloud. If you are a member of a church congregation, you may be asked to give a religious reading. Whatever you are reading, don't fall into the trap of thinking that reading aloud is easier than giving a talk because you don't have to remember the words. It is precisely because you have a script to read word for word that it can be *more difficult* than giving a speech. Reading from a script or book makes it more difficult to make eye contact and thus build up a rapport with the audience, hand gestures are awkward or impossible when holding a book or turning pages and involving the audience is harder too, unless the reading contains rhetorical questions. Therefore, when reading aloud, you must work hard to engage the audience.

Keep the following tips in mind:

- Choose something to read that is slightly shorter than the time-slot allocated. If the slot is ten minutes, choose a reading that lasts seven minutes. This gives time to introduce the context of your piece and for you to concentrate on reading slowly rather than gabbling to ensure you finish on time. At something like an Open Mic event, running over time is very bad manners, especially if other performers are on stage after you.

- If there is no allocated time, remember that audiences will tend to switch off after eight minutes or so. Leave them wanting more, not looking at watches and shuffling in their seats.

- Choose a piece that has a self-contained narrative arc (beginning, middle and end) without long description. If necessary, novel extracts can be edited in order to achieve this.

- Consider what medium you will read from. Using the actual book (if you are the author) gives good publicity as the cover faces the audience. But how is your eyesight? Avoid wearing reading glasses if possible – it hampers looking up from the script to include the audience. Have you edited the extract to better suit a live audience? In both of these cases it may be better to print the extract onto A4 sheets in a font to suit your eyesight. Printing has the added benefit that you can add 'stage directions' reminding you to look up, slow down or whatever. To avoid dropping the pages and mixing them up, stick them into a physical notebook or scrapbook. When printing the extract insert page breaks at a position to suit you rather than where they naturally fall, i.e. put the page break where there is a natural pause in the narrative so that you can turn the page during the pause rather than midway through an exciting part of the story.

- Practise the diaphragmatic breathing described in the 'Limbering Up' chapter of this book. Running out of breath is more obvious during a reading and can cause the ends of sentences to become quieter and without impact.

- Practise reading the passage as much as possible. Familiarity breeds confidence and will make it easier to look up and scan the audience whilst continuing to speak.

- Pretend you are an actor, step into 'performance mode' and add as much drama as possible to the performance. No one will complain about too much drama and feeling in a reading but they will complain if you mutter in a monotone to your shoes.

- If the passage contains dialogue, try to make the individual voices as different as possible. Consider turning your head to the right when speaking as one character and to the left when speaking as the other. Alternatively, take a step to the right and then a step to the left to indicate the two different characters. However, when using a microphone during a performance, be careful to keep your mouth within a constant range of it to avoid becoming inaudible as you move your head to switch between characters.

- Look up at the audience as you read, keeping your thumb running down the margin, so that when you look back at the page you haven't lost your place. Practise where you will raise your head and make coloured markings in the margin so that you can easily find your place again.

- Take a step backwards at the end of the reading to indicate to the audience that you've finished and it's time to applaud.

Learning Point: Reading aloud isn't an easy option and as much thorough preparation is needed as for a speech.

Exercise: Print your manuscript and mark appropriate

pauses and emphasis. Determine where you will make eye contact with the audience and mark it in the margin. Practise, practise, practise!

TO JOKE OR NOT TO JOKE

"If you want to tell people the truth, make them laugh, otherwise they'll kill you." – Oscar Wilde

Actors are told never to work with children or animals. Public speakers should be told never to tell jokes. Telling appropriate one-liners is incredibly difficult and best left to professional comedians. That said, a little bit of humour in a speech is essential. It lightens the atmosphere, builds audience rapport, makes the facts more memorable and keeps audience attention. The best humour comes from within your subject matter – you have been booked as a speaker, not a comedian. A speaker is aiming for wry smiles or gentle chuckles, not belly laughs.

How to Do Humour Without Jokes

- **Know Your Audience.** We don't all find the same things funny and we don't all speak the same language. A room full of millennials is unlikely to laugh at a funny reference to something that happened in the 1950s. A room full of octogenarians is unlikely to understand amusing references to the latest thing on social media. Think about what unites your audience and work on what they have in common.

- **Use humour safely.** Don't make the audience, or sections of the audience, the butt of your jokes. Some people may easily take offence. I once listened to an after-dinner speech by a prominent politician, who made a quip about a visit to a particular, less-prosperous, local area being like a visit to Beirut. He meant it to raise a smile but I found it offensive – there might have been someone from that neighbouring constituency in the audience.

- **No swearing.** Respect your audience and don't use language that you wouldn't use normally in polite company. Leave the blue jokes and toilet humour for the late night stand-up comedians.

- **Avoid contentious subjects.** Never try to be funny about religion, politics, sex, race or class. No speaker wants a riot on his hands!

- **Self-deprecation.** This is something the British are good at and gently poking fun at yourself is one of the safest types of humour. It will also get the audience on your side.

- **Experience it before poking fun.** Only make fun of situations you have experienced yourself. For example, only a wheelchair user has the right to tell funny stories about the trials of accessing disabled toilets and only a person who's gone through the trauma of chemotherapy can joke about the experience of hair loss and obtaining the right wig.

- **Collect funny material.** Trying to invent something funny to put in a speech is difficult. It's much better to collect humorous material before you need it. Note down anything funny you see in everyday life; it could be something said by a small child, a T-shirt slogan or an observation in a supermarket. Audiences like laughing at the everyday life we all have in common. A file of notes gives you humour to draw on when writing a speech.

When telling a funny story:

- Use expressive language and word pictures to paint the image in the mind of the audience.

- Keep the story uncomplicated and explain it in simple language.

- Ensure you signal the imminent arrival of the punchline by slowing down your delivery, inserting a pause and then emphasising the punchline. Warning: This requires practice.

- If no one laughs, don't panic! Either ignore the fact that no one laughed and carry on with the rest of your speech or, if you're feeling ultra-confident and feel you can carry it off, say something like, "Never mind, it seems our senses of humour don't match." Failing to raise a laugh isn't the end of the world and you will live to speak another day.

Learning Point: Humour in a speech is great but don't force it and don't gamble, if it might cause offence to even one audience member, don't say it.

Exercise: Brainstorm how you might inject a little humour into your speech without explicitly telling a joke. Practise delivering that humour with pauses in the right place.

IMPROMPTU SPEAKING

Would you like to say a few words?

An impromptu speech is given on the spot with no preparation. The ability to speak off the cuff in this way is very useful and there are many occasions we might be called upon to speak without notice, such as:

- Giving a vote of thanks to a visiting speaker. This requires impromptu speaking skills in order to pull together the best bits of the visitor's speech (even if it was poor) and to talk about them appreciatively.

- Putting a point of view in a meeting at work. This requires the ability to listen to the opinions of others and respond to them immediately.

- Chairing an event when things underrun and you may have to ad lib in order to fill the program.

- If you are an expert or have a strong opinion about something, you may be called upon at short notice to give a comment or explanation about something topical.

- An unexpected question at a job interview requiring a coherent answer on the spot.

- A colleague unexpectedly asks you for input during a high-level meeting.

- Answering audience questions after delivering a prepared speech. Some questions may ask for your opinion on a particular topic – a logically constructed answer backed by examples will show you to be professional and knowledgeable.

All of the above occasions, and more, require the ability to order thoughts very quickly and give a coherent, logical short speech. Many people make the mistake of thinking that because impromptu speaking is off the cuff and without prior warning, it can't be practised. It may not be possible to practise speaking on the exact topic in advance but you can regularly challenge yourself to speak off the cuff. Each day choose a random topic and force yourself to speak about it (out loud and standing up if possible) for two minutes. Open a dictionary or reference book at a random page and speak about the word or topic your finger lands on. Or write out some of the topics that you might be called to speak on, put them in a hat and draw one out at practice time. Rehearsing like this gets your brain used to quickly organising thoughts on random subjects. Alternatively, join a Speakers or Toastmasters Club – both give members regular practice at impromptu speaking (known as 'topics') in front of an audience. Website details for these organisations are in the Resources section at the end of this book.

The following tips will help if you're asked to speak off the cuff or give an impromptu comment or opinion:

- **Focus on the task.** Don't worry about what the audience is thinking. Don't think about your nerves. Focus solely on the topic about which you have to speak (easier said than done, I know!).

- **Repeat the topic.** When you are asked to speak, pause for a few seconds and then repeat the question or subject you've been asked to discuss, this gives you a few extra seconds to think about what you are going to say.

- **Start and end strongly.** As with a prepared speech, these are what the audience is most likely to remember. When you begin, speak clearly and make eye contact with the audience. Make sure that eye contact is still there as you make a definite conclusion to the speech.

- **Speak slowly and use pauses.** This makes more impact on the audience and requires less material to fill the allotted time.

- **Plan ahead.** In real life you are unlikely to be asked to speak at short notice on something you know nothing about. Think about subjects that are likely to come up in a meeting/Q&A session/interview or relevant topics that you could use as 'fillers' should you be chairing an event and prepare for them.

- **Keep up with current affairs.** This is particularly important within your specialist subject. Questions are most likely to arise on areas currently in the news.

An impromptu speech with no structure won't make any point or impact, it will simply be a ramble through the speaker's disorganised thoughts. There are a few well-tried structures which are worth carrying in your head for possible use:

- **Three Things.** Think of three things relating to the given topic and add a brief introduction and conclusion. For example, if the theme is 'Travel broadens the mind' think of three ways that this sentence is true or false – meeting new people, trying new food and seeing new landscapes – and then give a brief conclusion.

- **For and Against Argument.** Taking the travel theme again, present an argument for travel broadening the mind and an argument against travel broadening the mind. Conclude by indicating which of these arguments carries the most weight.

- **Past, present and future.** If the topic is the more general 'Travel', the speaker could take the audience on a brief journey through the history of travel, from horse and cart, through steam engines, cars and into the future of rockets and space travel.

- **PREP.** This method of speech construction is advocated by Toastmasters International. Make your **Point**, for example, 'Travel broadens the mind – this is absolutely true.' Give your **Reasons**, these could be similar to the points made in the Three Things structure above. Give one or more **Examples** to back up your reasons, if possible work these into a story to hold the attention of the audience. Conclude by reiterating the **Point** made at the beginning of the speech.

Learning Point: Impromptu speaking is an important skill and structuring these mini speeches should be practised regularly.

Activity: Consider an upcoming meeting or event and the topics that might arise. Prepare a brief outline of what you might say if called on. Alternatively, consider some hot topics within your specialist subject and how you might comment if asked.

POWERPOINT

"PowerPoint doesn't kill meetings. People kill meetings. But using PowerPoint is like having a loaded AK-47 on the table: You can do very bad things with it." - Peter Norvig, Google Director of Research.

The use of PowerPoint slides can enhance a talk and help the audience to remember the message or the slides can ruin the presentation with information overload and a presenter more concerned with his technology than his audience. Think about the tedious, slide-heavy presentations you've dozed through at work and compare that experience to occasions where the presenter has only a handful of meaningful slides and a bright, snappy delivery technique. Which presenter would you rather be?

The following points are designed to help you put together and present a talk strengthened, not dominated, by the use of PowerPoint:

- For each element in your presentation, think about whether the point can be explained in words alone without the need for a slide. If no slide is needed – great! If a visual is necessary think carefully about what will work best. A graph? A picture? A pie chart?

- Focus on the audience and the message you want them to take away. Unless you are a PowerPoint salesperson, you are not here to show off your knowledge and mastery of the software.

- Do not read your presentation from the slides. PowerPoint does not replace the need for thorough preparation and rehearsal.

- Slides are there to *support* the narration. Slides do not make the speaker redundant. The slides should be of little use without you there to explain them. Do not put the full text of your presentation on the slides.

- Don't squeeze too much information on each slide. Empty space makes the slide easier to read.

- Use the bullet point 6 x 6 rule. One idea per

point, up to six words per point, up to six bullets per slide. Have the points appear one at a time so that the audience can't read ahead.

- Don't give your slides a patterned background – it makes them difficult to read.

- Some of the audience may be dyslexic. For these people dark text on a pastel background works best, particularly dark blue text on cream.

- Too many special effects such as animations and text fly-ins get tedious.

- The best slides may have no words at all. The slide could be a hard-hitting image, for example, a starving child and the statistic 11%. The speaker could explain that 11% of the world's population is starving and then reveal the slide and pause whilst the audience absorb the impact.

- Avoid using cartoonish clip art. Most of it has been seen before and cartoons don't create a professional image. Use your own photos or professional stock photos but check out the associated copyright rules first.

- As the presenter, make sure you can see the slides as you speak without fully turning your back on the audience.

- Do not direct your speech to the slide. Speak to the audience and make eye contact. You are the star of the show, not the slide.

- Pause when switching to a new slide. This gives the audience a moment to study it without trying to listen and read at the same time.

- At points within the presentation regain audience attention by switching to a blank or black screen and speaking without slides. This will increase the spectators' anticipation and interest.

- Don't include anything in your slide deck for which you must apologise to the audience. If the text is too small enlarge it, try using a sans serif font such as Arial somewhere between 24 and 40 point. If the graph is difficult to understand, simplify it.

- Know how to move backwards through your presentation in case someone asks to see a particular slide again.

- Use a handheld wireless clicker to move from one slide to the next. If you are speaking at a large venue, check the clicker's wireless range.

- Have a backup copy of your presentation on a memory stick. If the event organiser is providing the computer, email them a copy of the presentation in advance as well. Belt and braces should always be the motto where technology is concerned.

- Be prepared for complete technical failure by being able to give the presentation without slides. For this scenario, it can be useful to take along printed copies of the key slides to be used as handouts if the talk can't be given without the audience having sight of particular graphs or tables.

Never forget that when using PowerPoint you, the speaker, still need to give a performance. You still need to engage the audience, influence them and tell them a story.

Learning Point: Fewer, cleaner slides = Greater impact.

Activity: Plan out the slides needed for your presentation following the guidance given above. Then see if you can cut the number of slides down further.

SPEAKING ENGAGEMENTS

Make speaking your business.

This chapter of the book is for those who wish to take their public speaking outside of the workplace, speakers club or family celebration arena and offer themselves as a speaker for hire to the multitude of groups and organisations that regularly use outside speakers.

Getting started

As an unknown speaker with no track record, start small and local. Be prepared to speak to very small audiences for no remuneration. Look upon each event as a learning experience and a chance to watch audience reaction to see what does and doesn't work in your performance. It's better to experiment in front of a few people rather than a packed hall. Start with any organisations that you, or your family, have a personal contact with and ask if you can use them as guinea pigs. Or ask at your local church if any of their organisations such as Mothers' Unions or men's groups would be willing to give you a try.

The Ground Rules

Before advertising yourself as available for paid bookings, work out the parameters you're prepared to work to. Some things to consider:

- The distance you are prepared to travel with/without travelling expenses and what expenses you'll charge, for example, the mileage rate if you're driving or the bus fare.

- Speaking fee. Be prepared to work for free initially, but as you gain confidence and experience try to make speaking for free the exception for particular small groups or special causes, rather than the rule. Working for free devalues your talk and also makes it harder for people who need to make money from speaking to charge a realistic fee. A compromise can be to donate your fee to a charity chosen by you or the group to whom you are speaking.
  If you want or need to make significant sums from your speaking, aim at the corporate/business market which often uses motivational speakers for staff training. Also,

think about joining the Professional Speaking Association (see the Resources section at the end of this book).

- What equipment you will need the venue to provide. Do you have your own screen and projector if you are using PowerPoint? Do you need a table to set out a display of objects? It is easier to find engagements if you don't have to rely on the venue to supply specialised equipment.

Finding Engagements

Try the following suggestions to get your first speaking engagements:

- Ask local hotels, golf clubs and other venues about the groups which hire their meeting rooms. Many of these organisations will use speakers.

- Some libraries keep a list of speakers to which local organisations refer. If your library has such a list, ask to be added to it.

- Contact the local county headquarters of the Women's Institute and ask about the procedure to be added to their speakers' list. In the West Midlands, where I live, it costs £15 to be added to the list, in other counties an audition may be necessary.

- Register your details on the Speakers' website http://www.diannemannering.co.uk. This is a directory of speakers covering a multitude of subjects from across the UK. It is free to join and also free for club secretaries to use when booking speakers. The website is aimed at speakers who charge only a modest fee and bookings secretaries with a small budget. Registration is done via an email to Dianne Mannering who will then create a page for you on the website.

- Register your details at https://speakernet.co.uk/. This site offers a similar service to the one mentioned above and is also free to use. I found the administrator of this site very helpful when I had difficulty uploading a photograph.

- Have business cards printed to distribute at each event – often people in the audience will be members of another group looking for speakers or have friends in a different group needing to book a speaker.

- Join Twitter and follow local groups. It's a good way of finding out what's going on in the area and what organisations exist. But remember, social media is about building relationships over time and networking – do not post a stream of 'Book Me to Speak' tweets.

Taking the Booking

Much of this is common sense but can get overlooked. It is sensible to draw up a 'booking template' and talk through it each time you are approached to speak.

- Get the full address and postcode of the venue, not just general directions. If you will be using satnav, ask whether the postcode works with satnavs or have people been known to end up in a field or at the other end of the village? This can be a particular problem in rural districts where one postcode covers a large area.

- Ask for a mobile number that you can call should you hit problems on your journey to the engagement.

- Check whether the organisation needs an invoice in order to pay you. Should this be sent in advance or taken to the event? If unknown expenses are involved can they be added in pen to the invoice at the event, for example, a car park fee?

- Be clear how long you are required to talk. Does this include or exclude questions?

- When agreeing the date always ask for the year – some secretaries book 18 months in advance and turning up a year too soon would be embarrassing! Buy next year's calendar well in advance to note down these bookings.

- Check the venue will be able to provide any equipment you need.

- Find out where you fit into the program for the whole event so you know what to expect.

- Depending on the type of talk you are giving, it might be wise to find out the audience's current skill level/knowledge.

- If you have your own books or anything else to sell, check that this will be acceptable. Warning – some places may take a commission. Take plenty of change with you and decide if you are happy to accept cheques.

- Ask how big the audience/venue will be. If it's large, ask if speakers are provided with a microphone. Remember a handheld microphone or one on a stand will restrict your movement and a clip-on microphone will require a waistband/belt to hold the battery pack and a lapel or front buttoning shirt/blouse for the microphone clip.

- If you would like to be introduced to the audience or billed in a particular way, for example, if your qualifications or experience are important to flag up your expertise in the subject, make sure you request this and give all the details when the booking is made. You might think it sounds big-headed but the chairperson will be glad to have facts on which to hang their introduction.

Before the Event

Don't leave anything to chance:

- Decide whether you need to tweak your standard presentation. Is it the required length for this booking? Can you focus the content to suit this particular group? Do current events have any bearing on your speech content? Will your gestures and movement need to be limited because of a microphone?

- Reconfirm with the person who booked you a few days before the event.

- Decide what you'll wear (and make sure it's clean!)

- Pack a bag with everything you'll need for the presentation.

On the Day

Stay cool, calm and collected!

- Be careful what you eat or drink immediately

before a speaking engagement. Salty food like crisps or nuts encourages the production of saliva and you may end up spitting at the audience. Chocolate and other dairy products can stick around the mouth. Carbonated drinks may cause hiccups. Ice cold drinks can be a shock to the system rather than a calming influence. It's safest to stick to a cup of tea!

- Arrive in good time. If you are part of an event where there are multiple speakers, try to listen to one or two of them before your slot – it will add an extra dimension to your own speech if you can link back to the earlier speakers.

- Take notice of the room you will be speaking in. If the room contains things which absorb sound, such as heavy curtains, a low ceiling or a lot of people, be prepared to project your voice more than usual.

- Be warm, friendly and animated to those who greet you. They will provide familiar faces for you to focus on when speaking.

- Chat to a few of the audience as they arrive. They may raise points you can elude to in the talk and will also provide more friendly faces during your presentation.

- Have some water to hand during the

presentation. If you have a moment of panic or lose your way, take a minute to have a sip of water and get yourself back on track. A pause to take a drink will not be seen as a weakness by the audience.

- Don't pick on people to answer questions – some people are happier not being expected to take part.

- If, during the presentation, people ask complicated questions which are likely to be of minority interest or may send your timing out, suggest you take the issue 'off-line' and discuss it afterwards.

- Similarly, if an audience member is being awkward over a particular point in your speech, don't show that you are annoyed or cross, stay calm and suggest you discuss the point after the presentation.

- Don't be insulted if people appear to be texting. They might be live tweeting about something you've just said!

- Don't be knocked off track if someone falls asleep during your speech. I've had this happen to me twice when speaking to groups of older ladies. The first time I was speaking immediately after a large lunch had been served. At the end I apologised to the organiser for having bored somebody to sleep. It was a great relief when I was told that particular lady always dozed off after lunch. The second time it happened was mid-morning and no food was involved but that organiser had warned me in advance about one lady who always fell asleep – and, sure enough, she did! Younger people have reasons for not keeping their eyes open too – they may have a young baby, be jet-lagged from a foreign business trip or have been studying late at night. However, if several people close their eyes you might want to look at the structure and content of your talk!

- If time for a Q&A session has been allowed at the end of your talk but no one raises their hand, be prepared to fill the silence by saying, "One of the questions I'm most often asked is ….." This can be where your impromptu speaking skills come in to fill the gap. Or, as a novice and if the event you're speaking at is open to the public, you can do as I did early in my speaking career: I planted a friend with a pre-prepared question in the audience at my local library. As it turned out, I didn't need her, the 'real' audience had plenty of questions but it was reassuring to have that backup.

- If you don't know the answer to a question, be honest and say so. Then throw the question to the audience in case anyone else knows the answer or offer to find out later and get back to the questioner.

- Always stay and chat until everyone's questions have been answered even if the formal event has concluded.

After the Event

Give yourself a pat on the back – you carried it off and survived!

- Many people are exhausted after giving a talk. This reflects the amount of energy that goes into giving a good presentation. Don't worry about it, just give yourself time to recover.

- Drop a note of thanks to the organiser.

- Some speakers go from an onstage 'high' to a post-event 'low'. If this happens to you, be kind to yourself and re-energise by planning your next speech.

- Give yourself a debrief. From the audience response to your speech, work out what did and didn't work and use this to improve your performance next time.

- Keep a record of the event, i.e. which talk you have given to which group. This will avoid the embarrassment of duplication if they ask you to speak again.

Insurance

You may want to consider whether your public speaking activities require insurance cover. This might be to cover any equipment that you use as part of the presentation (laptop, projector etc.) or to cover you from legal action should someone trip over your bag or be otherwise injured through your actions. There is an insurance recommendation on Dianne Mannering's website (mentioned earlier in this section) and it may be worthwhile searching out further professional advice.

Learning Point: Taking on speaking engagements is like running a small business and should be done professionally with precise recordkeeping so that you turn up at the right place at the right time and have a record of your earnings to supply to HMRC for tax purposes.

Activity: Draft a business plan for your speaking business, including how you will attract bookings and how you will keep diary and financial records. Create a template to use when taking a booking for an engagement.

THE VOTE OF THANKS

The purpose of a vote of thanks is to thank a speaker (usually a guest speaker) on behalf of the audience. A vote of thanks can be a daunting task for three reasons:

- It follows an established speaker who has been invited especially for the occasion.
- It is partly an impromptu speech because it requires comment on a speech which has only just been given.
- The vote of thanks is often the last thing on the agenda and the audience might be restless and eager to get home.

As the person designated to give the vote of thanks, you must pay attention to the chairperson's introduction of the guest speaker and also listen carefully to the whole of the guest speaker's speech. It may help to make brief notes during the proceedings of anything you might refer to in your vote of thanks.

Basic Template for a Vote of Thanks

- Introduce yourself. Most of the audience may know who you are but the guest speaker may not.

- Explain that it is your pleasure to be offering the Vote of Thanks on behalf of the club/society/audience.

- Highlight two or three points from the guest speaker's presentation that you found particularly relevant, useful or important.

- Conclude by thanking the guest speaker and invite a round of appreciative applause from the audience (if this is appropriate to the occasion).

- If your Vote of Thanks is closing the whole event, make any comments appropriate to the whole event, then wish the audience and the speaker a safe journey home.

Things to Avoid in a Vote of Thanks

- Do not ramble. A Vote of Thanks is not a speech in itself. It should not regurgitate the contents of the guest's speech. A Vote of Thanks should be 3 – 4 minutes MAXIMUM.

- Do not include a list of thanks to other people who might have been involved in organising the event. Thanking these people is the job of the chairperson. Including those thanks here will detract from the thanks being given to the guest speaker.

- Do not physically address the Vote of Thanks solely towards the guest speaker. Speak to the whole audience, glancing at the guest speaker occasionally. Everyone should hear and be included in the eye contact of your speech.

- Don't be tempted to prepare the Vote of Thanks in advance. The Vote of Thanks should reflect what is actually said on that occasion by the guest speaker. It should be 'off the cuff' and short.

A Fictional Example of a Vote of Thanks

Good evening ladies and gentlemen. My name is Sally Jenkins and it is my pleasure to give the vote of thanks to our guest speaker, John Smith, on behalf of Anytown Civic Society.

John, I really enjoyed your speech. Your memories of scrumping apples as a schoolboy in the manor house grounds were particularly amusing. Next time I visit the gardens, I will look up and imagine you hiding in the apple tree branches.

On a more serious note the point you made about conserving our heritage for future generations was very important and something we should all think about actioning.

Finally, thank you for sharing the pictures of the restoration work currently going on at the manor house. I know I'm not the only one grateful for the vast amount of effort put in by that army of volunteers.

I'm sure the audience would like to join me in showing their appreciation of your speech. (Start the applause).

Optional – All that remains is for me to remind you all that our next meeting is in a fortnight's time and wish everyone a safe journey home.

Learning Point: An effective vote of thanks requires good listening and some note-taking skills, as well as the ability to speak in public.

Activity: Next time you attend an event with a speaker, mentally or on paper, prepare what you would have said, had you been giving the vote of thanks. At home practise delivering your version of the vote of thanks.

PANEL EVENTS

"For me, conferences are like little mental vacations: a chance to go visit an interesting place for a couple of days, and come back rested and refreshed with new ideas and perspectives." – Erin Mckean, founder, Wordnik.com.

Many conferences and events have moved from single speaker sessions to panels. A panel is usually made up of a chairperson and three or four panel members. The panel members have a common interest or experience which the chairperson will invite them to share with the audience. The session will begin with the chairperson introducing each panellist and giving them a short time to address the audience. When all the panellists have spoken, the chairperson will usually open up to questions from the audience so that a discussion can take place. The typical physical setup is with the panellists sat in a row behind a table at the front of the room or on a stage, but there is a move towards more 'relaxed' settings using tall stools, sofas or other types of furniture.

The points below will guide you whether you are the chairperson or a panellist. Re-read the quote from Erin Mckean at the top of this chapter- whatever your role on the panel, aim to send delegates away having learned something new, whether it be hard facts or simply a different way of looking at the world. However, do check with the event organiser in advance exactly how things will run and what is expected of you. Not all panels will be run the same way and you may have been invited onto a particularly innovative one!

Chairperson

- If possible have a chat with audience members just before the event to find out where their interests and questions lie.

- Once the event starts you are in charge and it's up to you to ensure everyone gets a fair chance to speak and things don't run over time. You may need to diplomatically interrupt a panellist who is rambling.

- Research all members of the panel in advance so that you can give them a brief introduction and know where their strengths and experience lie for directing the questions.

- Make sure the conversation stays with the panel rather than involving yourself. The chairperson is not there to share his or her opinion.

- Move the discussion on if any of the panellists begin to self-promote.

- Refocus the discussion if either panellists or audience comments go off at a tangent.

- Never relax when the panellists are speaking. The chairperson must keep on top of any debate or questions and ensure the audience gets their money's worth.

- End the session by inviting the audience to show their appreciation of the panellists with a round of applause.

Panellist

- Research the other panel members prior to the event and think about what you will be able to add to the conversation that is outside of their experience.

- Find out from the organiser and/or chairperson any particular topics or angles they would like to include in the discussion. Is there a specific objective for the panel? What is the level of expertise of the audience? Are there any rules about or opportunities for promoting your book/product/service?

- Once you know what is expected regarding subject matter/slant/time restrictions etc., prepare your introductory contribution.

- Arrive at the event early in order to chat with the chairperson and other panellists.

- Stay focussed during the discussion and avoid superficial comments that add nothing of value for the audience. Don't go off topic.

- Add something new to the discussion rather than merely agreeing with and paraphrasing the other panellists. Bring in something from your own experience to add weight to your words.

- Try to make the panel a lively discussion by questioning the other panellists and building on what they've said.

Unfortunately, audiences don't usually go into panel events with very high hopes of finding them useful. This was highlighted in "The Panel Report: A 2014 Snapshot on the Effectiveness of Panel Discussions at Meetings, Conferences and Conventions" from Powerful Panels. According to the report, panels are often seen as a 'lazy' format at conferences; the organiser throws a few people together and leaves them to get on with it. Panel chairs are often seen as ineffective in directing a worthwhile discussion. Bear this in mind – taking part in a panel discussion is not an easy option compared to taking to the floor on your own!

Learning Point: Chairing a discussion or being a panellist requires much preparation in the same way as preparing a speech. In some ways it is more difficult than a speech because you don't know exactly how the discussion will go.

Activity: Imagine you've been invited to an event in your specialist area as a panellist. Plan your initial address to the audience so that they know your background and stance on the subject to be discussed.

1 MINUTE NETWORK INTRODUCTION

"If you want to go fast, go alone. If you want to go far, go with others." – African Proverb.

Fear of the one-minute networking introduction is something that brings many new members to my local speakers club. We don't give specific advice on this type of presenting but these entrepreneurs find the general speaking experience offered by the club is sufficient to build the confidence they need to promote their businesses more effectively.

The following tips on giving short networking presentations can be used as a building block on top of the general speaking skills covered so far in this book. Even those who don't attend networking events may find it useful to have a one minute pitch of this kind up their sleeve. The pitch might be for a favourite charity, an amateur sports team in need of a sponsor, a book in need of shelf space in the local shop or a local club looking for new members. It's surprising the influential people we come into contact with at the most unexpected moment - don't get caught out without a pre-prepared elevator pitch!

- Have a brilliant beginning that focusses on the benefits your business brings. For example, a hairdresser might say, "I give people the perfect crowning glory and they leave my hair salon full of confidence." But don't be too obscure – make it plain what your business is!

- Keep the presentation focussed on a particular point. Don't try to include everything you do. This might mean talking about one specific example of how you've helped a client or tying a current news story to your business or linking your business to a particular statistic. The aim of the networking presentation is to spark an interest rather than do a hard sell. Those who want to learn more can chat with you afterwards.

- Don't go into the history and minutiae of your business unless it is of particular relevance to the case study, accolade or example that you are talking about.

- Highlight the benefits your business brings to

its clients. For example, if you offer a guaranteed twenty-four-hour turnaround in dry-cleaning, emphasise that your customers never have to worry that they won't have the right outfit ready for that last minute business meeting or social occasion.

- Vary your one minute of content at each meeting.

- Include a call to action. This might be as simple as liking your Facebook page or it might be something more specific such as asking for an introduction to a particular company or individual who may be able to help your business.

- State your name and company name at the end of your presentation. People will make more of an effort to remember it if you've already sparked their interest and given them a reason to want to remember you.

- Keep it natural by smiling and speaking in a friendly manner. Adopt the same attitude when others are making their presentations. People prefer to connect with those of a friendly, empathetic disposition.

- Prepare well. Others may look like they're speaking easily and naturally off the cuff but, as in all public speaking, what you see is only the tip of the iceberg compared to the amount of work that's been put in.

- Networking meetings and clubs vary in their tone and requirements. Take note of how your peers speak and the content they use and then adapt your presentation for next time.

Pam Collins is a senior group leader for Utility Warehouse and attends a Business Network International (BNI) chapter. She says, "We don't sell to the room but want to highlight why people should remember us and want to refer us to the people they meet. Personal stories are always good, as are visual aids. Visual aids also mean that people are not looking at you for the whole time! Asking for a referral to a specific industry, company or person works better than a more general request."

Learning Point: The one-minute networking introduction must hook the audience at the beginning, stay focused and end with a call to action.

Activity: Draft a networking introduction or elevator pitch and get feedback on it from family, friends, co-workers or your speakers club. Accurately time how long it takes to present your pitch.

WEDDING SPEECHES

For many people a wedding is one of the few times they will need to speak in public and, very often, fear will spoil the whole event. The fear is completely unfounded. The wedding speaker's audience is one of the best possible; relaxed, happy, amongst friends and family and without huge expectations of a great oration. Everyone is willing to let mistakes by nervous speakers pass over their heads. There may be the odd family feud that drops negativity into the gathering but, as a speaker, put that to one side and give the bridal party the speeches they deserve.

Wedding speeches aren't simply formalities at the end of the wedding breakfast. When carefully crafted these speeches can give guests an insight into the happy couple, add amusement to the proceedings and get the rest of the celebrations going with a swing. Most weddings no longer stick to the old etiquette of who is and isn't allowed to speak at a wedding. When I married, thirty plus years ago, the speakers were always predominantly male – bridegroom, best man and father of the bride. It was almost unheard of for a female to speak but now it's quite acceptable for the bride (think Meghan Markle) or bride's mother to address the gathering.

This chapter is split into sections covering each of the possible speakers at a wedding. If you've been asked to speak but don't fit into any of the sections then I hope by reading the whole of this chapter you'll get some guidance on the content and style of your speech.

The speeches are usually given at the end of the wedding meal (traditionally called the wedding breakfast) after dessert has been served. However, it is becoming more common for the speeches to be given prior to the food being served so that the speakers can then relax and enjoy the meal and the rest of the reception. In addition to the people listed below, there may also be a Master of Ceremonies (MC) introducing the speakers and making sure everything runs smoothly.

The purpose of wedding speeches is to thank those who need thanking, to wish the bride and groom well and generate goodwill and smiles amongst all those present. It is advisable that all those speaking consult with one another to ensure that all the necessary thank yous are included without duplication and that special mention is made of any guests who have travelled a great distance or otherwise made a great effort to be there. No guest should go home feeling overlooked whilst someone else was mentioned three times. It's also wise for all speakers to share the running times of their speeches with each other to ensure that guests won't be forced to endure two hours of talking or that it won't all be over in five minutes flat! As a rule of thumb, no single speech should last more than seven or eight minutes.

If wedding etiquette is particularly important to your occasion, it may be beneficial to consult a more specialist publication for the rules regarding a formal wedding. This chapter is designed only to help improve the speakers' performances.

Toast to the Bride and Groom

The father of the bride usually gives the toast to the bride and groom but this could be done by a close family friend or the bride's mother. In this age of single parents, divorce, blended families and marriage in later life (when our parents may already be deceased), it is increasingly common for this toast to be made by someone other than the bride's birth father.

The purpose of this speech is to welcome and thank all the guests for coming, with particular reference to the groom's family. The speaker should talk about the bride and her new husband and then ask all those present to raise their glasses in a toast to the bride and groom. There is room for some gentle humour in the speech.

Suggested format (aiming for a length of around six minutes):

- Introduce yourself – there may be guests at the wedding who haven't met you before.

- Welcome and thank the guests for coming. Mention any individuals who have made a great effort to be there and also anyone who hasn't been able to come.

- Mention any 'housekeeping' necessities, for example, any rules regarding smoking, photography, social media posting (the bridal party may want to be the first to post any pictures), bar closing times, running order etc.

- Welcome the groom's family and thank them where necessary for their contribution to the smooth running of the wedding.

- The central part of the speech should be about your daughter, the bride. If the bride's mother will not be making a speech, ask for her memories and thoughts to include in yours. Include some or all of the following (if you are not the father of the bride, adapt this as necessary):
  - o Memories of the bride growing up.
  - o Times you have felt most proud of her.

- o Times she made you laugh (keep this tasteful and positive so the audience is laughing with you and your daughter and not at her).
- o Her positive character traits.
- o Anything you have learned from her.

- Welcome the groom into the family. You might mention:
  - o His positive character traits.
  - o Any memories of first meeting him.
  - o Any positive influence he has had on your daughter.
  - o Why you feel he and your daughter will have a strong partnership going forward.

- Optionally, share some wisdom with the bride and groom about what makes a long and happy marriage. This is particularly appropriate if you have enjoyed a lasting marriage.

- Propose a toast to the bride and groom.

Toast to the Bridesmaids

The bridegroom usually responds to the toast to the bride and groom and traditionally closes his speech by toasting the bridesmaids. It is also acceptable for the bride to make this toast or for the bride and groom both to speak (although not generally in unison!).

The purpose of this speech is to thank those who have

helped with the wedding preparations, thank the best man and any other supporters of the groom, thank the bridesmaids and thank the groom's parents. The groom should also praise and speak positively about his new wife and vice versa if the bride is speaking.

Below is a suggested format if the groom is making the speech. Adapt the suggestions as required if the bride is speaking.

- On behalf of yourself and the bride, thank whoever made the 'father of the bride' speech.

- Make the other required thank yous:
  o All the guests for coming.
  o The bride's parents (especially if they have contributed financially towards the wedding – don't be specific, just mention their generosity).
  o The groom's parents for his upbringing.
  o Best man and any groomsmen (this can be done with humour – possibly relating to the stag night).
  o Bridesmaids.

- Praise your new wife and say how much she means to you. Possibly mention your first meeting or anything else significant that's happened whilst you've been together. You will be referring to her as 'my wife' for the first time – so make the most of it! The audience (and your new wife) will appreciate a little bit of romance in your speech at this point and make sure you look the bride in the eye as you say how much you love her.

- Propose a toast to the bridesmaids.

- Briefly introduce the best man or equivalent prior to his or her speech, mentioning how you know each other.

Best Man's Response on Behalf of the Bridesmaids

A best woman, matron of honour or another member of the bridal party could speak instead of or as well as the best man. Being chosen to be a best man or woman is a great honour and places a lot of trust in you. Make sure you live up to this honour but don't stress about it too much – you are among friends!

As with all that has gone before in this book, preparation is the key to a great speech. The speeches which appear most relaxed and effortless are usually those that have had the most preparation. Bear in mind the following points when preparing:

- Give some thought to the mix of guests. A room full of elderly relatives will not enjoy a plethora of blue jokes.

- Talk to some of the groom's other friends to get anecdotes for your speech. Disregard both the most salacious tales and the tamest ones, choosing those that will raise a laugh without making anyone listening feel uncomfortable or embarrassed.

- Don't talk about the groom's exes – it may be appropriate to refer to them on the stag night but not on the day he is pledging himself for life to one woman.

- Include tasteful compliments on the appearance of the bride and bridesmaids.

- Give an example of how happy the bride makes the groom or how well suited they are as a couple.

- Make the whole audience feel part of the speech by including something from the groom's childhood or commenting generally on his personality. Relying solely on tales from your student days together will shut out the majority of the guests.

- Think about possible visual aids, for example, an enlarged unflattering photo (possibly poster size so that everyone can see) from the groom's childhood or maybe a favourite toy supplied by the groom's mother.

- Practise pausing before delivering the punch line to a funny story.

- If, after reading this book, you're still terrified

of giving the best man's speech try finding safety in numbers. Ask a couple of the groom's other friends to deliver parts of the speech with you.

The format of the best man's speech will depend on the relationship between the groom and best man and how long they have known each other or what the best man can discover about the groom's early years. Having a format to start from is a great help to novice speakers and the one included below is suitable for a best man who knows/can find out something about the groom's childhood. The chronological format of the speech makes it simpler for the speaker to remember and easier for the audience to follow:

- If the groom hasn't already done so at the end of his speech, introduce yourself and explain how you know the groom.

- Talk about the groom's childhood. Any starring roles in the school play/football team? Funny sayings? Imaginary friends?

- Talk about teenage years/early adulthood. Learning to drive stories? Part-time jobs?

- Best man's personal experiences of the groom.

- Meeting of groom and bride.

- Become serious and talk about the fine

qualities of the groom, how they've influenced you and how these will ensure his happiness with the bride.

- Compliment bride and bridesmaids.

- Read out any messages of goodwill from absent friends and family.

- Finish by proposing a toast to the happy couple.

There are many examples of best man's speeches to be found on the internet. Read or listen to them and see which format best suits your situation.

Advice to all wedding speakers

Use bullet-pointed notes on index cards so that you don't forget anything. Talking freely around each bullet point will produce a more natural delivery than reading from a full script. If you lose your thread, have a sip of water whilst you collect your thoughts. If nerves mean you do have to read the speech, read as slowly and clearly as you can with plenty of pauses to allow the audience to take in your words.

Learning Point: Wedding guests will be in a celebratory, happy mood and won't judge the speakers in the same way as a more formal audience might. Prepare your speech thoroughly and then enjoy it!

Activity: Write the wedding speech you've been asked

to give and then condense it into bullet points so that you can talk freely around each point.

PARTIES AND CELEBRATIONS

Every celebration needs a speech.

No celebratory knees-up is complete without a speech to mark the occasion and to recognise the life and achievements of the guest of honour. Recently I have spoken at an eightieth birthday party and at an event to mark fifty years of service for the tower captain at the church where I am a bell ringer. The way I crafted my speeches may be useful to others with a family birthday or other anniversary on the horizon.

In both cases I structured my speeches chronologically to make them easier for me to remember and easier for the audience to follow. I went wide and inclusive with both speeches by including references to the music or current events that accompanied milestones in the guests of honour's lives.

Eightieth Birthday Speech

We all have our own musical 'era'. It's usually the pop tunes that played on the radio and in the discos or dancehalls of our late teens/early adulthood. Similarly, music can take us back instantly to a particular holiday, a theatre trip or maybe a romance in later life.

With this theme in mind, I asked the octogenarian for the musical milestones and associated memories in her life. I then crafted a speech around this. The speech connected with the audience because they knew the songs I was talking about. Instead of just reeling out a list of private family memories over the guest of honour's life I had 'gone wide' so the whole audience could relate to what I was saying and felt included. It was the icing on the cake when the DJ was able to play some of the songs mentioned in the speech at the disco that followed.

In a similar vein, it would be possible to journey through someone's life by mentioning the cars they'd owned at significant times or the important current events that formed the backdrop to a person's life path. This way, even if some of the guests didn't know the party host as a young man or woman, there are parts of the speech everyone can relate to.

Fifty Years of Service Speech

I tackled this speech by looking at the dilapidated Minute Book from the bell ringers' committee meetings of fifty years ago. I read aloud significant extracts from the book relating to the Tower Captain's ringing career and I tied these to current events from

127

that time, giving the audience something 'wide' to relate to as well as the minutiae of the Minutes. I finished the speech by talking about the Tower Captain's fine qualities that had made him so successful. I then invited other (pre-warned!) guests to add their own memories and plaudits. Having several people speak *briefly* can hold guests' attention more than one long speech.

Tips on some other types of standard party speeches are below. The rule of thumb is to ensure that all the people who need thanking are thanked, praise the guest(s) of honour and in all cases try to include something that even new friends of the host can relate to.

Retirement Speech

Sooner or later most of us will have to say a few words to our work colleagues as we transition from employee to 'retired' status. It's easy on these occasions to take a very long walk down memory lane and speak for far too long. Limit your speech to around ten minutes and include something to interest all those present, for example, advice to younger people building their careers, shared memories for older colleagues and a little bit about your plans for the future for everyone. Pay tribute to those who've made your working life easier and more enjoyable. End by saying what you'll miss about working and what you hope will make up for that in retirement. Use bullet point notes so you don't forget anything and practise!

Christening Speech

A christening or naming ceremony speech is a little unusual in that it will mean nothing to the little individual at its centre but it will be of value to the youngster's family and the other guests. The speech should thank guests for coming and mention the significance of the ceremony that has just taken place. Talk about the loving family the child has been born into and give a special mention to any siblings so that no one feels excluded. Ponder the possibilities for the baby's future and remind everyone present of the duty they have to help the family ensure that the child's formative years lead to a successful future.

Engagement Speech

The engagement party speech is less onerous than a wedding speech but should express similar sentiments. It aims to celebrate the couple's recently announced commitment to one another. An engagement speech could be given by any of a number of people: the couples' parents, friends, siblings or the couple themselves. The suggested framework for whoever makes the speech is: Introduce yourself if there are guests present who don't know you, thank the guests for coming and mention anyone who's made a significant contribution to the event. Share one or two anecdotes about the engaged couple, perhaps how they first met and then comment on their good qualities and how well suited they are. Toast the future of the happy couple.

Wedding Anniversary Speech

The milestones of a long marriage will give much content for an anniversary party speech. If, as the speaker, you didn't know the couple at the start of their relationship, do some research amongst the family about their early years together. Along with the usual thanks to the guests and short anecdotes about the couple, mention each partner individually and the good qualities each has brought to the long-lasting relationship. Give some context to the speech by tying milestones in the marriage to significant news events of the time. Props, such as enlarged old photos or something from the original wedding, will add interest. Don't forget to wish the couple many more happy years together and finish with a toast.

Learning point: Taking a speech 'wide' by including current events and popular culture draws the audience in, even if they don't have close personal knowledge of the family or person involved.

Activity: Brainstorm ideas for how to take your speech wide and make it relevant to everyone, as well as including the personal milestones important to the guest of honour. A chronological speech will be easier to memorise and deliver.

THE EULOGY

Many people fear public speaking more than death.

A eulogy is a speech given at a funeral or memorial service and celebrates the life of the person who has died.

When asked to give a eulogy it's common to be overwhelmed by a range of emotions and fears. The eulogy is an important part of the funeral or memorial service and therefore you may feel flattered to have been given this honour. For the same reasons you may be absolutely terrified of making a bad job of it. Depending on how close you were to the deceased you may be worried about how to speak without breaking down in tears. The lack of time to prepare the eulogy before the funeral takes place may also cause you to panic.

Take a deep breath, a blank piece of paper and calm down by brainstorming ideas for the content of the speech. Bear in mind that the average eulogy is around five to ten minutes long. If you are not the only one speaking at the service then it may be considerate to make your speech shorter and to coordinate with the other speakers to make sure you don't cover the same ground.

The following three points are designed as signposts to creating a logical and meaningful eulogy at a time when you may be feeling upset and overcome by the many other tasks that have to be accomplished when someone dies.

- Pull together the basic biographical information on the deceased. Dates of birth and any marriage. Births of children. Career highlights.

- Talk to the close family and friends of the deceased and ask for a memory. Do this even if you are planning the eulogy for your spouse or partner – work colleagues or football mates will have seen a different side to the deceased. The various stories may have a common theme which you can highlight in the speech, for example, a love of animals, generosity of spirit or a wicked sense of humour. It is unlikely anyone will come forward with a bad story, if they do then it should be ignored – a eulogy isn't a place for airing past grudges. People are likely to be generous with their stories and there may be too many to include in a five to ten minute eulogy; therefore it's polite to warn people that you won't be able to mention every story but they will all help you gain a better understanding of the deceased.

- Organise the content into a logical fashion that will be easy for the congregation to follow, this would usually be chronological.

A simple structure for a eulogy could be:

Introduction

- Acknowledge the occasion. "We are here today to remember and celebrate the life of John Smith."

- Many people at the funeral may already know you but still introduce yourself in case someone from a different facet of the deceased's life has never met you. "My name is Joe Bloggs and I've known John since our student days at Anytown University."

Middle

- State when and where the deceased was born and mention his or her immediate family. "John was born in London during the cold winter of 1962. His sister Susan had just started school and was besotted with her new baby brother. John's father was a PE teacher and his mother ran the local playgroup."

- Include any childhood memories that have been passed to you.

- Move onto the deceased's marriage or the beginning of their life with a long-term partner. Also mention any children and grandchildren. "John married Mary in 1986, a wonderful wedding that several of us here were privileged to attend. Their children Sue, Sam and Simon were born over the next ten years and, from witnessing the family together, I know John was a great dad who loved his children dearly. He was very excited a couple of months ago when he told me that Sue was expecting his and Mary's first grandchild."

- Include two or three short memories or stories here. Humour can be used but it should be sensitive and appropriate. "One of John's hobbies was church bell ringing. He was a valued member of St Peter's ringers because of his patient tuition of new ringers and also because, apparently, he did a wicked impression of Quasimodo which always had everyone in stitches."

- Talk about the deceased's achievements and passions. "John was a self-disciplined, determined individual who always gave 100%

to everything. He became Master of the Anytown bell ringers, manager of the Anytown supermarket and published three novels. But above and beyond all that his family always came first."

End

- Try to end the eulogy by describing the influence that the deceased had on you and how that will continue going forward. Try to make this have meaning for the whole of the congregation. "John taught me to never let failure get me down. His mantra was 'if at first you don't succeed, try, try, try again'. I know that I am not alone in thinking that John was an inspiration to young and old alike. Going forward, when we find ourselves in a difficult situation I'm sure many of us will ask ourselves, what would John have done in this situation? And then act accordingly."

- Say a final goodbye to the deceased. "Rest in peace, John."

- Or you may wish to end with a short poem, written by a family member if possible, or a meaningful quote.

Once the script for the eulogy is complete, ask a close family member of the deceased to review it and check it for accuracy and appropriateness. The aim of the eulogy is to honour the dead not embarrass the living in any way.

Delivering the Eulogy

- Practise as much as possible before the funeral/memorial service. Do this standing up, projecting your voice and imagining there is an audience in front of you. Time the speech to ensure it fits the slot you've been given.

- If possible, before the service ask to stand where you will be delivering the eulogy to get a feeling for the room and what it looks like.

- It's acceptable to have notes – this is an emotional occasion and no one expects you to be word perfect. However, try to be as familiar as possible with your material. Print your notes in a font large enough to read easily.

- Try not to be nervous. Most of the congregation will be admiring you for taking on a job they would be unable to do.

- Speak slowly and make eye contact with all corners of the room. This will draw people into what you are saying.

- It doesn't matter if you show emotion. If anything this will add authenticity to your words. If emotion causes you to lose your place, pause and take a moment to regather your thoughts.

Advice from a professional

Andrew Bulman is a qualified civil funeral celebrant working across central England. The advice he gives on delivering a eulogy is hard to beat and he's given permission for me to reproduce it here:

Before I trained as a funeral celebrant I considered myself an excellent public speaker and assumed that the skills required for delivering a keynote speech at a conference or presenting a report about a young offender in a Magistrates' Court, which is where I had learned to speak in public, would be transferrable to the task of delivering a eulogy. To a degree, my assumptions were correct but, in undergoing training to be a celebrant, I was made aware of some very key differences and have learned to apply them.

In my experience the effective delivery of a eulogy can be summarised in 4 P's:

> 1. Pace
> 2. Projection
> 3. Poise
> 4. Practice

Pace

The pace of delivery is critical, and you have to teach

yourself to speak slowly. People attending a funeral, especially those most directly affected by the death, are in a particular emotional state, where listening and comprehending become more challenging. A normal reading pace is likely therefore to prove to be too fast for mourners to properly take in what you are saying. The rule of thumb is to attempt to deliver 100 words per minute and to ensure that there are clear pauses between sentences and paragraphs. Most funeral ceremonies, especially cremations, are time limited, and the whole ceremony needs to be done and dusted within a period of between 30 and 45 minutes, including allowing 5 minutes at the beginning and the end to get people in and out of the chapel. To that end, if you assume there will be some music or a hymn and a reading or a prayer, plus some words at the point of the formal committal of the coffin, a eulogy needs to be no more than 10 minutes long and more usually no more than 8 minutes long. So, any eulogy more than one thousand words long will either have to be read too quickly to be properly understood or will cause the ceremony to overrun if read at a proper pace. The latter scenario is likely to land the funeral director with a fine which will not please them.

Projection

It goes without saying that you need to make sure your words are heard properly, so volume and diction are important elements of delivering a eulogy. However, the size of the audience may differ significantly, requiring you to adjust your approach. Funeral audiences may well also contain a number of older people who have hearing difficulties and effective projection and erudition are the best means of enabling everyone to hear your words and feel a part of the ceremony. There may be audio equipment, microphones and a hearing aid loop system etc. there to assist you (ostensibly) but, in my experience they can sometimes add to the challenge, because you have to stand uncomfortably close to the microphone for it to pick up your voice which feels unnatural and constraining, so be aware of this. There will almost certainly be a lectern on which you can place your written eulogy and it is absolutely essential that you raise your head and look at the audience when you speak. Being able to look down at your written text and look up again to deliver the words at regular intervals is a skill worth developing and you may find annotating your text in some way to ensure your eyes return to the correct section each time is a useful pre-delivery exercise.

Poise

If you watch people delivering speeches at public events, they tend to move about and use their hands and arms for emphasis; the use of the body in this way helps make the delivery somehow more dynamic and interesting. This was how I would approach a speech at a conference for example. However, when I trained as a celebrant I was told to stop moving because it was too distracting. When I looked at video of myself I had to agree, and I had to force myself to stand still and not move my hands at all. In many ways this remains the hardest challenge for me with regard to delivering a eulogy. Fortunately, the availability of the lectern means you have something you can grip which forces you to keep your hands still and if you are gripping the lectern you are not really in much of a position to move the rest of your body! I'm getting better however at standing and reading with my hands behind my back which I think is the most dignified method.

Practice

Whatever else you do, do practise reading your eulogy aloud several times and if possible involve a third party as a critical friend. Pace, projection and poise can be tested out and tweaked, but most of all reading aloud helps you spot poor and potentially challenging phrasing in advance to ensure that on the day you are word perfect. If at all possible make the effort to practise delivering your eulogy at the actual venue, so you get a sense of the acoustics and the physical layout of the auditorium. You cannot afford to stumble over your words. This is someone's funeral you are speaking at and, in the audience, will be people who are feeling desperately sad and seeking comfort in a ceremony that properly reflects the life and character of their loved one. It needs to be perfect every time. You must not treat the task of preparing and delivering a person's eulogy with anything but the greatest respect each time.

Further useful information on funerals can be found on Andrew's website:
www.andrewbulmanfuneralcelebrant.com.

Learning Point: Delivering a eulogy requires a different approach to other types of public speaking and it is also one of the few times when reading your speech is acceptable.

Activity: Write the eulogy and practise reading it aloud slowly with a timer. Ensure it comfortably fits into the allotted time with a safety margin to allow for problems on the day.

WHEN IT GOES WRONG

Murphy's Law: "Anything that can go wrong will go wrong."

Despite Murphy's law, most things don't go wrong but even the best public speaker will suffer occasions when things don't go according to plan – remember Theresa May's speech to the Conservative Party Conference in 2017 when she was presented with a P45, suffered a coughing fit and letters fell from the words on the stage backdrop behind her?

In such circumstances the most important thing is to keep your composure and your sense of humour, don't let the audience see that you are rattled. When the speaker appears calm and in control, the audience feels comfortable too. If something bad does happen to you, here are some tips for recovering the situation and getting the speech back on track.

Running Out of Time

This may be because the speaker before you exceeded their time slot. Or on arrival you were asked to speak for a shorter time than previously agreed. Or you misjudged how long your speech would take once any audience participation was factored in. Or the time shortage could have been caused by one of any number of other things.

If you find yourself running out of time, do not speak faster and faster in the hope of cramming everything in. The audience won't get the gist of what you are saying and will pick up on your panic. Neither should you simply chop off the conclusion of the speech because to stop suddenly will appear odd and you will lose any planned call to action. Instead, omit some of the less important points of your speech, points which aren't crucial to your overall message. Only you know exactly what you were going to say and so only you will know you've missed out parts of your presentation. It's easier to drop parts of a speech or shorten them on the hoof if you have internalised rather than memorised the speech. Internalising means you can speak on the same topic in different ways.

A Blank Mind

Everyone goes blank from time to time and the audience too will know what it feels like to suddenly lose the thread of a conversation.

Take a few seconds for a drink of water to regather your thoughts. Or recap to the audience what you've already said in order to find your place. Don't be afraid to admit that you've forgotten what you were saying – the audience are often willing to remind you of the last point made and that will prompt you for what comes next. As mentioned above, the audience doesn't know exactly what is in your speech so if you miss something or go through it in a different order they won't know.

Microphone Stops Working

If it's a very large venue there's little you can do in these circumstances except hope the event organiser has a backup plan. In a smaller hall, encourage the audience to move forward as close to you as possible. Similarly, as the speaker, you should get as near to your listeners as possible. Shut any doors or windows that may allow noise to drift in and compete with your voice.

Hecklers

Unless you are a politician or speaking on a controversial subject you are unlikely to get heckled. The British public is well known for its reserve! Hecklers usually have their own reasons for wanting a share of the attention which is rightfully yours.

If you do get heckled, remember that as the speaker you are in charge of what happens. Don't argue or interact with the heckler. Tell them you will be happy to address their points, one-to-one, after the presentation. As a last resort, if the presentation is being spoiled for the rest of the audience, the heckler should be asked to leave.

Don't let one bad experience steal your confidence and prevent you from speaking in public again. As humans we have a tendency to magnify our failures and play down our successes. You may have felt that the speech went badly but your audience may have been unaware of your difficulties. The speaker will compare his performance to the 'perfect' vision he wanted to project. The audience has no such vision and if they learned something or were entertained, they will be happy.

Learning Point: The better prepared a speaker is, the fewer things will go wrong. All speakers have tales to tell of performance mishaps but often the audience won't notice.

Activity: Internalise and bullet point your speech instead of learning it by heart so that you are better able to recover from time allocation shrinkage, a blank mind or interruption by hecklers.

RESOURCES

Organisations

Association of Speakers Clubs

'Become a better speaker, better presenter and better leader.'

I can personally vouch for the effectiveness of clubs affiliated to the Association of Speakers Clubs (ASC). The atmosphere is friendly and supportive. Every speech given by members is constructively evaluated so the speaker knows what he or she did well and what can be improved on. There are no instructors or teachers, everyone in the club takes a turn at speaking (both prepared and impromptu speeches), evaluating others and chairing meetings. In addition, joining the club committee or getting involved with running the ASC at Area, District or National level will further improve your confidence and leadership skills. For speakers who want a greater challenge than speaking within the club, the ASC runs annual speech, evaluation and topics (impromptu speaking) competitions which culminate in a national final at the ASC conference.

To find a club near you visit:
http://www.speakersclubs.uk/.

Toastmasters

Toastmaster meetings run in a very similar way to those of the ASC, i.e. a learn-by-doing environment in a non-threatening atmosphere. The main difference is that Toastmaster members can also follow a formal leadership training program.

To find a club near you visit:
https://toastmasterclub.org/.

Professional Speaking Association

The Professional Speaking Association has several levels of membership and is aimed at the speaker who is making or hoping to make a living from their speaking. Professional level members must be proposed for membership by two existing members who have heard them speak. Associate membership is open to anyone with an interest in professional speaking. The PSA does not teach public speaking skills but associate members can attend events and mix with and learn from professional speakers.

To find out more visit https://www.thepsa.co.uk/.

Independent Speakers Clubs

Some towns have independent speakers' clubs which are not affiliated to any national body. Some of these clubs may have been part of the ASC or Toastmasters International in the past and still be run on similar lines. Other clubs may have a particular slant, for example, they may specialise in business presentations. An internet search will highlight any independent speakers' clubs in your area.

Books

Public Speaking for Writers by Alison and Malcolm Chisholm. This book starts by explaining how to prepare your voice for public speaking and goes on to discuss obtaining bookings and delivering the speech.

The Art of Public Speaking by Dale Carnegie. This book contains many pages of material for reading aloud in order to practise changes of pitch, tempo, emphasis etc. A useful resource if you don't mind the rather old-fashioned style of the prose.

Public Speaking for Authors, Creatives and other Introverts by Joanna Penn. This book contains specific tips for introverts but much of it is applicable to anyone. I have heard Joanna speak and she presents with energy and enthusiasm.

Online Resources

Study about the amount of gestures used in TED talks: https://www.scienceofpeople.com/hand-gestures/

The Panel Report: A 2014 Snapshot on the Effectiveness of Panel Discussions at Meetings, Conferences and Conventions: https://powerfulpanels.com/2014-panel-report/

OTHER BOOKS BY SALLY JENKINS

Fiction

The Promise
A man has been stabbed. A woman is bloodstained.
The Promise is a psychological thriller which explores
the lengths to which people are prepared to go in
order to protect those they love and the impossibility
of ever fully escaping our past actions.

Bedsit Three
A girl has been buried in a shallow grave. Rain starts to
wash away the earth covering her. Every mother tries
to do her best for her child. But sometimes that 'best'
creates a monster. You decide whether the evil within
Ignatius is nature or nurture.

A Coffee Break Story Collection
36 short stories. Enjoy tales with a twist, competition-
winning prose and gentler slices of life, with a hint of
romance.

NonFiction (available on Kindle only)

Kindle Direct Publishing for Absolute Beginners
How to publish your first ebook on Amazon Kindle.

Walk the Cleveland Way
A short book designed to help walkers planning a
holiday on the Cleveland Way

Printed in Poland
by Amazon Fulfillment
Poland Sp. z o.o., Wrocław